FINDING
AN
ACADEMIC
JOB

*This book is dedicated to the bravest
person I know, the person whose unfailing love
and encouragement gave me the confidence
and the courage to persevere—
my mother, Bernice Sowers.*

—Karen Sowers-Hoag

*To my former students who have gone on
to become successful academicians and to
future students who will continue in this
very rewarding career path.*

—Dianne F. Harrison

FINDING AN ACADEMIC JOB

Karen Sowers-Hoag
Dianne F. Harrison

GRADUATE SURVIVAL SKILLS

SAGE Publications
International Educational and Professional Publisher
Thousand Oaks   London   New Delhi

For information:

SAGE Publications, Inc.
2455 Teller Road
Thousand Oaks, California 91320
E-mail: order@sagepub.com

SAGE Publications Ltd.
6 Bonhill Street
London EC2A 4PU
United Kingdom

SAGE Publications India Pvt. Ltd.
M-32 Market
Greater Kailash I
New Delhi 110 048 India

Printed in the United States of America

Library of Congress Cataloging-in-Publication Data

Sowers-Hoag, Karen M.
  Finding an academic job / by Karen M. Sowers-Hoag.
    p. cm. — (Graduate survival skills)
  Includes bibliographical references and index.
  ISBN 0-7619-0400-X (acid-free paper). — ISBN 0-7619-0401-8 (pbk.
: acid-free paper)
    1. College teachers—Employment—United States—Handbooks,
  manuals, etc. 2. College teachers—Selection and appointment—
  United States—Handbooks, manuals, etc. I. Harrison, Dianne F.
  II. Title. III. Series.
  LB2331.72.S68 1998
  378.1'2'02373—dc21   97-45245
This book is printed on acid-free paper.

98 99 00 01 02 03 10 9 8 7 6 5 4 3 2 1

Acquiring Editor:	Jim Nageotte
Editorial Assistant:	Corinne Pierce
Production Editor:	Sherrise Purdum
Production Assistant:	Denise Santoyo
Typesetter/Designer:	Danielle Dillahunt
Indexer:	Mary Mortensen
Print Buyer:	Anna Chin

CONTENTS

SERIES EDITOR'S INTRODUCTION

Not only is there an art in knowing a thing,
but also a certain art in teaching it.

—Cicero, 46 BC

The Sage Series on "Graduate Survival Skills" would not be complete without a volume addressing the topic of finding an academic job, inasmuch as a large proportion of graduate students ultimately hope to teach in their field. You, the reader, are fortunate in that two immensely talented academics have prepared this book, *Finding an Academic Job*, because each author has considerable experience in the hiring of new faculty. Both Karen Sowers-Hoag and Dianne F. Harrison are deans of schools of social work at the University of Tennessee and at Florida State University, respectively, who each year interview numerous applicants for assistant professor positions, and in some cases actually offer them coveted tenure-track positions. As such, each author is well positioned to lend her expertise to the subject matter of this book.

Individual chapters deal with preparing one's job application credentials, finding the right type of position to apply for, applying for a job, interviewing, and negotiating the job offer. Other chapters deal with the problems and advantages of dual career families, and how to obtain a nonacademic position if your first-choice options do not develop. I believe that recent and soon-to-be finished graduate students will find this volume an immensely practical guide.

Academic positions, particularly full-time ones leading to tenure, can be among the most rewarding and enjoyable ways of earning a living and professing one's vocation. Job-finding skills are essential for a successful career. Unfortunately, these skills are rarely formally communicated to the graduate student. If you are lucky, a thoughtful professor will exert some effort on your behalf, but rarely will you find course work or even less formal workshops dedicated to assisting you in the job search process. Sowers-Hoag and Harrison have distilled their many years of faculty recruiting experience into this book. It is a treasure trove of practical suggestions and details in the search process that are all-too-easily overlooked.

BRUCE A. THYER
THE UNIVERSITY OF GEORGIA
ATHENS, GEORGIA

PREFACE

We have targeted this book toward individuals seeking first-time employment as full-time faculty in colleges or universities, also known as *the academy*. We based our thinking and writing on our combined 35 years of experience in higher education institutions, public and private, large and small. We have conducted research in the area of faculty hiring since 1982, and are familiar with hiring issues both from the literature and through first-hand observations of the hiring process. We approach this topic from the perspective of academic administrators (as deans), giving advice to graduate students and new PhD graduates who desire to be faculty. Our positions have given us insight into this process from the standpoint of having hired new faculty, as well as assisting graduate students secure their first academic appointments. These collective professional experiences form the basis of our suggestions about job search strategies. Although we recognize that there are no guarantees in the job market, we believe that the guidelines offered here will prove useful to new faculty candidates. We have tried to be candid, and probably have been too frank about some of the idiosyncrasies of the academic market. Although there are certain discipline-specific nuances in the job search process, most of the advice given here is relevant across disciplines and academic fields. We sincerely welcome reader comments and feedback. We are grateful to both past and present colleagues and our own PhD graduates who continue to seek our advice.

1

WHAT COLLEGES AND UNIVERSITIES LOOK FOR IN NEW FACULTY

This book is designed to provide useful information and guidelines to doctoral students seeking their first academic appointments as full-time instructional faculty. Much of the advice and guidance offered here is relevant to other types of academic positions as well, such as part-time faculty, academic administrators, and senior-level faculty. The information contained in these pages is intended to help you become more competitive in the academic marketplace.

WHAT'S SO GREAT ABOUT BEING A PROFESSOR?

The prospect of a degree of job freedom that is unusual by other job standards is what attracts most people to the academy (Rosovsky, 1990). Colleges and universities give you the freedom to think, say, and research almost whatever you choose. Except for scheduled class times and committee meetings, your hours are largely left up to you. This is not to say that as faculty you do not work long and hard. In fact, if you become a faculty member at a college or university, you will typically work more than 40 hours per week. Yet it is entirely up to you to schedule your out-of-class and out-of-department business time as you see fit. Engaging in academic discussions, keeping abreast of current literature (through reading and attending professional conferences), talking informally with students, running labs, conducting research, providing public service and consultation, and writing up the results of that research for scholarly publications are some of the ways that unscheduled time can be spent. Although faculty in both public and private institutions are increasingly being held accountable for their productivity and teaching loads, an academic position is still one of the best jobs in the world.

As faculty, you can expect not only to enjoy relative freedom in your schedule but to be surrounded by a community of teachers and scholars where a spirit of inquiry and interest in knowledge and learning exist. Academic politics aside, philosophical differences and debate are essential and exciting components of the academy. In addition, each year a new group of mostly energetic and enthusiastic students presents itself to challenge you and to reinvigorate the academic environment. The United States has arguably the best system of higher education in the world. Other countries routinely send their most outstanding and brightest students to our colleges and universities to be educated; as faculty, you have the opportunity to share ideas with them.

It should come as no surprise, then, that the majority of PhDs across disciplines aspire to the faculty life. These preferences exist in spite of the fact that in some disciplines, notably in the humanities, faculty salaries are regrettably low. In other areas such as law, business, medicine, and social work, faculty salaries can be competitive with some nonacademic counterparts.

WHAT ARE YOUR CHANCES OF
BECOMING A PROFESSOR?

With so many people interested in an academic career, you may well be asking what are your chances of landing a suitable position. Faculty applicants over the next decade will find themselves in a seller's market, with the universities being the buyers (Chronister & Truesdell, 1991). Faculty shortages began during the mid- to late 1990s, and are projected to continue into the next century. These shortages are the result of what has been termed the *graying of the professoriate.* In the 1960s, the higher education system began turning out many more PhDs than ever before in response to the Kennedy administration's push for better education. The consequent retirements now, coupled with increased student enrollment projections as the baby boomers' children enter college, give you an excellent opportunity to have an academic career (Gill, 1992).

In 1989, The *Chronicle of Higher Education* reported that "colleges and universities will need to hire 37% more professors in the year 2003 than they have for the coming academic year." The *Chronicle* further noted that "an especially acute shortage of faculty will occur in the years 1996, 2000, and 2003" (Mooney, 1990, p. A15). A substantial excess demand for faculty in the arts and sciences has been predicted during this period (Bowen & Sosa, 1989).

Given these anticipated faculty shortages, why would anyone need a book on how to get a faculty job? One reason is that many faculty candidates enter the job market severely underprepared for the process—naive, at best. Unfortunately, existing university structures do not always allow the time necessary for faculty to serve as mentors to help a student increase the likelihood of a successful job search, and applicants will want to maximize the chances of landing the best position available.

Despite the growing need for good faculty candidates, and despite the truism that the "good people will always get jobs," there are situations where departments simply leave faculty vacancies open if the applicant pool has been judged as weak or unimpressive. Positions can also be held vacant if a department is not able to hire its first- or second-choice candidates because those candidates were hired elsewhere. Often, several universities will compete for the same pool of top candidates. Some faculty and academic administrators subscribe to the approach that it is better not to hire at all than to hire a second- or third-choice applicant. This is especially true in institutions where salary dollars from vacant faculty lines can be used for other purposes in the budget. As a result, even in an era of faculty shortages and increased competition among higher learning institutions for faculty candidates, you may

find yourself at a disadvantage from a hiring perspective for a variety
of reasons having to do with the university's need to find the best "fit"
between its needs and candidates' qualifications.

THE FIT BETWEEN YOU
AND THE INSTITUTION

The degree of fit between you and the particular job position involves
both the match between the specific areas of expertise needed by the
department and the match between the department and the institution's overall set of priorities. For example, at a private institution
where faculty are essential to departmental survival, evidence of skills
such as teaching, fund-raising, grant writing, community-based research, and community service abilities and an expressed eagerness to
continue in such activities would represent a good match between the
institution's priorities and the candidate. A particular research agenda
and teaching interests that correspond with those being sought would
represent another match. Bringing additional characteristics, such as
bilingual skills or educational experiences that match the employing
institution's needs, represents yet another type of match.

There is more to the search process, however, than just the
institutions' needs. The search process is a two-way street down which
both you and the institution ride looking for the best possible match.
For you to understand this process better, it may help you to understand some of the variations you will run into during this search so
that, as you analyze your personal preferences, needs, and qualifications, you can begin to define more specifically what institutions you
will want to pursue.

HOW COLLEGES AND
UNIVERSITIES MAY DIFFER

At the most simplistic level, new faculty need to be teachers, scholars,
and good departmental citizens (i.e., do a fair share of departmental

work, get along with others; Kogan, Moses, & El-Khawas, 1994). The degree of importance of each of these attributes (i.e., how they are weighted or evaluated) may differ considerably from one institution to another, however.

For instance, there are differences in the types and sizes of institutions: college or university, undergraduate liberal arts or research-one university, predominantly teaching or research mission, public or private, small (less than 5,000), medium (5,000 to 10,000), or large (over 10,000). Different types and sizes of institutions often look for different characteristics or credentials in faculty hires. A small 4-year liberal arts college might want to see the range of courses you have taught during your doctoral program and evidence of good teaching skills, followed by your service experiences and commitments. Service could be the assumption of departmental committee work, heavy advising, or even some form of administrative assignment; other service activities could involve community outreach such as volunteering to judge science or art fairs. Much farther down the list of qualities sought at this type and size of college would be evidence of your potential as a researcher/scholar.

In contrast, at a research-one institution, graduate education and research represent important elements of the institution's mission ("research-one" refers to universities that have met certain criteria for such designation; sample criteria include having awarded a particular number of doctoral degrees within a specified time and having received a predetermined amount of external funding for research purposes). As a result, to be considered for employment at this type of university, you will need to demonstrate potential as a researcher/scholar. At a research-one institution, in contrast to a small liberal arts college, if you have little or no evidence of potential as a scholar, even excellent teaching skills will not make you a highly attractive faculty candidate. Although your credentials and qualifications in this area will be among the most important (if not the most important) qualities sought, they may not be sufficient to ensure getting the position you want. In the past, an outstanding scholar or researcher could get by on publications, research grants, or other evidence of scholarly or creative activity. Because teaching is increasingly held in high esteem even by research-one universities (Dalbey, 1995; Whitfield & Weaver, 1991), however, you will need to be prepared to show evidence of your teaching skills (or potential for such) at such a university. Indeed, for either type of institution, teaching will probably be an important part of your duties. It is very difficult to be hired anywhere if you carry evidence of less-than-satisfactory teaching skills, even though you may have been a brilliant scholar in your doctoral program or may show promise of being a future research star (Whitfield & Weaver, 1991).

In the following chapters, we explore the many issues and variables associated with your job search. In Chapter 2, "Preparing Your Credentials Early," we discuss the importance of carefully preparing yourself and your credentials for your job search. We go into detail about how to establish a track record, beginning at the time you enter your graduate or doctoral program, that will make you attractive to the institutions to which you apply. This includes assessing your own personal interests, talents, and career goals; ensuring that you teach as often as possible during your graduate work and obtain good course evaluations for the experience; beginning the process of publishing or performing creative and research efforts; presenting papers at conferences; becoming involved with grant writing; becoming a good academic citizen and colleague; and beginning to form a professional network that can help you in your job search.

In Chapter 3, "Matching Your Credentials and Preferences to the Job Market: Finding the Right Fit," we look at how you can use the information in Chapter 2 to establish the best fit between you and the institution of your choice. We discuss possible institutional characteristics you will want to consider and the kinds of institutional support you should look for. Then we suggest ways of analyzing your personal characteristics so that you can match yourself to an institution.

Chapter 4, "Your Search and Preparing Your Portfolio," has to do with the actual preparation of your portfolio. We discuss the importance of the timing of your search, and talk about traditional and electronic search methods and networking. We also give you tips on the preparation and presentation of your application materials, that is, the cover letter and curriculum vitae, and references so that you can make it past the institution's "paper" screen and move on to the more personal interviews covered in Chapter 5.

In Chapter 5, "Applying for and Getting the Position," we try to give you an idea of what to expect in the personal interview process, including possible screening procedures: telephone, computer, video-conference, or face to face. We also discuss the on-campus interview with its colloquium, class seminar, individual interviews, and social events, and offer suggestions on how to survive attacks by the local curmudgeons. We offer tips on how to dress and how to act to maximize your chances of impressing the search committee and faculty at the institutions to which you apply.

Chapter 6, "Negotiating a Job Offer," explores what to do during the time between the on-campus interview and your acceptance or rejection by the institution, a time when you may feel the stress of the job hunt very keenly. We provide information on what to do when you get an offer from someone, and how to negotiate the terms of employment. We also discuss how to decline the offer gracefully if you decide you do not want it.

Chapter 7, "Dual Career Issues," takes up the issues of dual career couples. Certain complications arise when you are searching for an academic position and your partner also has a career (whether it is in academics or some other field). Chapter 7 looks at these issues and makes suggestions about how you might overcome, or at least minimize, the difficulties inherent in trying to find employment for two.

The epilogue, "What If You Can't Find an Academic Position?" presents options to consider if you are unable to find a good fit between you and a college or university.

SUMMARY

An academic career can be exciting and fulfilling, and we feel that you should pursue it if you are interested in the level of job freedom and intellectual stimulation provided there. Due to the graying of the professoriate, the coming years will be an excellent time to pursue this kind of career, but you need to be well prepared to maximize your chances of obtaining the position you want, where your qualifications, needs, and preferences are optimally matched with the institution's qualities, needs, and preferences. Many nuances associated with the searching, screening, and hiring processes in the academy are examined in detail in the following chapters. It is our hope that the information provided here will ease the way for you.

2

PREPARING YOUR
CREDENTIALS EARLY

The best time for you to begin preparing for the academic job market is at the beginning of your doctoral or graduate studies. An overall strategy for this preparation should include setting two priorities: 1) obtaining the doctoral degree, and 2) establishing a track record that will appeal to employing institutions. These priorities are certainly not mutually exclusive. Institutions are hesitant to hire a candidate who is ABD (all but dissertation), and many require that you complete the doctorate before the beginning date of your contract. Although your track record is essential, the completed doctorate will give you an important competitive edge.

Job candidates often do not begin paying serious attention to their job credentials and track records until they begin dissertation work. This could be a mistake. To begin establishing your track record, you need to start assembling your portfolio or collection of your best work as soon as such materials become available throughout your doctoral program. Most of the highly competitive and very successful job candidates, those who eventually end up with several good job offers, appear to have paid as much attention to establishing their track records as to obtaining their doctoral degree. In this chapter, we focus on the kinds of activities and evidence that will ensure that you have a strong application portfolio by the time you are in the job market.

ASSESSMENT OF PERSONAL INTERESTS, TALENTS, AND CAREER GOALS

New faculty need to be teachers, scholars, and good departmental citizens, and universities and colleges may place different values on these activities depending on the size and mission of the institution. In preparing for your role as new faculty, you may want to assess (with the assistance of supervisory faculty) your interests, talents, and career goals. This assessment should be continuous throughout your doctoral program. You may find that your interests change over time as you grow during your doctoral studies and are guided by your mentors. You may also discover new and different talents as you meet the challenges of your course work.

Excellent teaching and scholarship are not mutually exclusive. In fact, the majority of good scholars and researchers are also good teachers. The reverse does not hold, however, that is, good teachers are not necessarily good scholars. Different people have different talents and interests: Not all chemists have Nobel prize potential or ambition, nor are all English doctorates excellent teachers by nature. Therefore, it is fortunate that universities and colleges have very different faculty needs depending on their size and mission, and so differences in future faculty talents and interests can also be accommodated. If you are very qualified and competent as a scholar and researcher and have less interest in teaching, you should seek out universities in which research is a primary mission. If you are more interested and talented in the classroom, you should probably focus on institutions that have primarily a teaching mission.

This is not to suggest that unqualified and untalented doctoral graduates can eventually find a faculty position if they just find the right college. Rather, to receive attractive job offers and ultimately a successful and satisfying career, you need to assess your interests and talents realistically and accurately, and match these with your future employing institution.

ESTABLISHING YOUR TRACK RECORD THROUGH TEACHING

If you have not yet mastered the art of good teaching, you have time to work and improve your skills by beginning the preparation of your teaching credentials early (Feld, 1988). As mentioned above, not everyone is born a good teacher. To become a good teacher, you need time, determination, and good faculty role models. As a starting point for establishing a track record that will appeal to future employing institutions, you should seek out teaching opportunities and spend as much time in the classroom during your doctoral studies as possible, as long as it does not inhibit your progress in completing your degree. In some universities, you may have relatively easy access to the classroom, that is, you may be assigned your own separate courses to teach or be assigned to a faculty member to assist in a course. Take advantage of these opportunities; they are invaluable to future employers.

In the not-so-distant past, most doctoral students were given a course assignment (usually an introductory-level course), handed a syllabus, and generally left on their own until the course was over or until some major problem arose that resulted in students complaining to academic administrators. Thankfully, most universities now have formal training and mentoring programs in place that will provide you with constant guidance and feedback. Some of these programs may videotape class sessions, allowing you and others to observe your classroom performance. Take every advantage of such programs, and give yourself the opportunity to mold and sharpen your teaching skills prior to entering the job market (Sowers-Hoag, Harrison, & Dziegielewski, 1989).

If such formal programs are not available, you can request advice and critiques from supervisory faculty, doctoral student peers, and students in your classes. Another suggestion is to spend time carefully observing and absorbing the teaching methods and styles of excellent teaching faculty. These informal methods of acquiring teaching skills may not be ideal, but, with time and determination, you can teach yourself to teach.

The particular teaching qualities and experiences universities and colleges are looking for in a candidate vary idiosyncratically from year to year, depending on retirements, resignations, and terminations within departments. Being able to market yourself in more than one teaching area increases the possibility of appealing to at least one institution. Therefore, another very important part of establishing your track record in teaching is to teach as diverse an array of courses as you can. Having a narrow, focused topic of study is necessary for research and dissertation work (although extremely narrow topics can also be problematic in dissertations), but such narrowness can be deadly in your preparation for the job search. This is especially true if you are interested in working in smaller, liberal arts colleges. If you are certain to be employed in a large department where ultraspecialization is the norm and faculty are never expected to teach broader foundation courses, then narrow teaching experiences and preferences might not be a problem. The difficulty, of course, lies in guaranteeing yourself, from the beginning and throughout your doctoral career, that such a possibility will occur. Therefore, you should probably opt for career "insurance" by making sure your credentials include evidence of teaching ability (and preferably experience) in at least two areas. In most disciplines, the ability to teach introductory as well as advanced courses is desirable. If at all possible, provide yourself with teaching experiences that will appeal to a broad array of institutions.

According to your particular interests and talents, you might teach one course in a narrow, advanced specialization topic, that is, one that is close, if not identical, to your dissertation topic and perhaps suitable for master's level study. The other course could be a broader area or foundation course at the undergraduate level. In social work, for example, you might have a substantive area of specialization and teaching such as the treatment of children who have been sexually abused, and also a foundation course such as research methodology.

This would permit you to apply to institutions that have openings in either child welfare or research methodology areas.

In both the physical and the social science areas, interdisciplinary teaching (and research) represents another type of teaching credential that could set you apart from a candidate pool. It is becoming more desirable, even in universities that focus on research, for faculty to be able to teach in more than one area. If possible, see if your institution will allow you to teach or engage in research in departments outside your PhD program to broaden your appeal when you go on the job market.

ESTABLISHING YOUR TRACK RECORD THROUGH COURSE EVALUATIONS

Another element of a candidate's track record related to teaching is course evaluations. Having satisfactory evaluations by students or faculty mentors can be extremely valuable in your portfolio. Prospective deans or department heads do not want an ineffective or problematic instructor on their faculty (especially if other qualified candidates can produce evidence of effective teaching), and good course evaluations can help persuade them in your favor.

The best kind of teaching evidence to include in a portfolio is some type of standardized measure, usually in the form of a university-based course evaluation summary. Also valuable are faculty observations of your teaching, notice of any teaching awards or honors, course outlines or syllabi, and, lastly, perhaps a few unsolicited student letters. Student letters should be used with caution, however. If too many are included, the portfolio may look "padded." You might opt to include a few (three to five) letters noted as "sample student letters," with an indication that additional letters are available on request. Some faculty who evaluate the portfolio, however, may view any positive student letters as having been "creamed" from the lot. Obviously, this may be quite accurate! The point here is not to go overboard, that in fact, letters from former students may or may not make that much of an impression on search committees and other faculty.

ESTABLISHING YOUR TRACK RECORD
THROUGH PUBLICATIONS AND PERFORMANCES

Publications in peer-reviewed journals; performances in the performing arts areas; and, in some fields such as English or history, book manuscripts constitute the best evidence of a research (or creative activity) track record. When your portfolio includes an established record of research and publication, you are clearly at an advantage, especially among those seeking positions in research universities.

Although the type and quantity of publications or creative activities that will impress future employers are very discipline specific and, to some extent, driven by institutional mission, the fact remains that you should begin in the very first semester of your doctoral program to establish a track record. Every paper written and every professional work effort throughout your doctoral program should be considered a possible publication opportunity. At a minimum, you should use papers prepared for courses as one source of possible publications.

It is probable that you will be assigned to work with faculty throughout your program of study. When possible, this work should also serve to contribute to your publication track record. Different disciplines have somewhat different procedures and mores about including students as authors on faculty projects, and unfortunately some faculty will take advantage of a student's talents without offering to include his or her name on the work. You should at least inquire about the possibility of inclusion to enhance your portfolio when possible.

Given the time that it takes for some manuscripts to appear in print (over a year in some instances), the sooner manuscripts are submitted for publication, the greater the likelihood that you will have publications in print by the time of your job search. The book *Successful Publishing in Scholarly Journals* (Thyer, 1994) is a very useful practical guidebook to help in developing your track record as a publishing scholar.

ESTABLISHING YOUR TRACK RECORD
THROUGH PAPER PRESENTATIONS

Presentations of papers and abstracts at professional conferences are another method of establishing a track record in research. Here, too, the more presentations prior to the job search the better. Not only do presentations add to your demonstrated record, they also provide opportunities to attend conferences, learn the ropes about such meetings, and begin building professional networks. These networks can serve you well during the job search (and, in some cases, throughout your career).

Because screening interviews for faculty frequently take place at such conferences, it is a good idea for you to attend and experience a conference before the job search. These conferences can be intimidating and even overwhelming to newcomers; experience can help you create a degree of comfort and confidence (and enjoyment) that you might otherwise miss.

It is also helpful to plan to have a presentation or be on the program at the conference at which you will be interviewing. This is an excellent way both to demonstrate your current professional activity and future potential and to offer prospective employers a visual reminder of you through the printed program listing. You should be aware, however, that in most fields, articles published in scholarly journals are awarded far more "weight" than conference presentations.

A CAUTION ABOUT RESEARCH TOPICS

You should keep in mind that your area of study or research topic(s) can either help or hinder your job search. Most doctoral students select an area of study early in their doctoral program and then settle on their research topic by the time of the dissertation, if not sooner. Such choices are influenced by a number of factors, including personal interests, faculty expertise and direction, and funding availability. Ideally, the selection of a research topic would be based fundamentally on the principles of academic freedom and the true need for knowledge development in an area. Unfortunately, this is not always the case. In fact, once you enter the job search, the marketability of your topic to future employers becomes an important issue. At a minimum, you need to be aware of possible reactions on the part of some future employers regarding your selection of research topic. Although you can appreciate your topic as offering a fresh perspective, others can interpret it as weird, unusual, or offensive. Similarly, an extremely focused topic can be seen as too narrow, or comprehensiveness viewed as too broad. If you have not considered the possible reactions to and even biases against certain areas of or approaches to research before your job search, your ability to respond to questions or criticisms may be lessened.

It is unfortunate to have to consider the reactions of future employers when you are making choices about research topics. Realistically, however, you may find that you have not made the first cut in your job search solely because of your research agenda. Because this is of such obvious importance to your future as an academic, you will probably want to consider possible negative reactions to your research topic before committing a large amount of your time and energy to it. Then, if you decide to go with a "riskier," more controversial topic, you at least will have made an informed decision.

The kinds of topics that may be red flags to search committees seem to be very idiosyncratic, yet can also be a function of current events and time period, faculty and societal politics, and institutional mission, all of which cut across disciplines. For example, in the not-so-distant past, faculty candidates who focused their research agenda on gender issues or ethnic minority studies were considered out of the mainstream, and therefore not as desirable, by some institutions. Although some biases have lessened, others have surfaced (or remain). Research on sexual orientation, racial differences in intelligence and abilities, creationism, extraterrestrial beings, and euthanasia is considered too controversial in some institutions. Even though there has been somewhat of a backlash against political correctness in society and in the academy, to a large extent, "research correctness" is alive and well.

Whatever your final decision on your research topics, we urge you to get feedback and guidance from supervisory faculty prior to making final topic selections. Feedback should routinely occur as part of the dissertation committee's responsibilities. You should ask specifically, however, that it speculate on the marketability of your topic above and beyond the significance of the topic to your particular discipline.

ESTABLISHING YOUR TRACK RECORD THROUGH GRANT WRITING

Along with publications, another kind of research evidence that will help you establish a good track record is grant experience. Writing or helping to write grant proposals, working on funded projects, and experiencing the research and grant process from beginning to end are all activities that help demonstrate research skills and, more important, future potential as grant-seeking faculty members and scholars. In research universities, especially in private research universities, the ability to secure external funding is a necessary skill not only for hiring but for later promotion and tenure. Too often, doctoral students seem to take the attitude that their own efforts to secure external funding should commence after they have their first job or their own lab. Unfortunately, if this is your attitude, that delay immediately puts you at a disadvantage in regard to other candidates who have made the effort to obtain funding while doing graduate or postdoctoral work. Start establishing your track record early if you want to be hired by this type of university.

A track record in grant writing can come from work on a faculty member's grant or project or from your own dissertation grant or fellowship. If you are in the physical sciences or psychology, your department may have a system set up specifically that addresses this need. Virtually all physical science PhD graduates do postdoctoral work for a few years in the laboratories of prominent scientists (some in private business or industry; Sheldon & Collison, 1990). This work is completed before they begin their academic job search. These experiences serve multiple purposes, including helping the new scientist learn additional skills and establishing a research and publication record. Often, during postdoctoral studies, new PhD graduates will set up their own labs and begin their own research programs, including securing grants to support their work.

In some disciplines such as psychology, where the academic job market is especially competitive, some doctoral programs form a sort of in-house postdoc, allowing recent PhD graduates to gain additional teaching experience and work on grant proposals and publications prior to their academic job search (Klesges, Sanchez, & Stanton, 1982). If you are not in a profession that formally supports PhDs with grant writing opportunities, you should certainly inquire in your department if opportunities for grant writing experience are available among faculty, to maximize your chances of being hired.

ESTABLISHING YOUR TRACK RECORD AS A GOOD DEPARTMENTAL CITIZEN

Another area in which you can prepare your credentials early (and wisely) is that of good citizenship. In some departments, citizenship is considered part of service duties in terms of the faculty assignment of responsibilities. Furthermore, most prospective employers believe that problem students ultimately become problem faculty (if they become faculty at all). Unless you possess some skill or attribute that simply cannot be found in any other job candidate, most universities will bypass potential problem individuals in their search for the good citizen. Therefore, it will be helpful for you to know what makes a "good citizen."

A good citizen will agree or volunteer to serve on committees, or take on tasks that need to be done but are not necessarily at the top of everyone's list of preferred things to do. Sometimes, a good citizen will take on thankless tasks that, if left undone, might create problems, but are bothersome to complete, such as updating the department's bylaws and mission statements.

A good citizen will get along well with colleagues, will be cooperative and sociable, and will be willing to handle a fair share of departmental chores. A good citizen will not act like a prima donna (i.e., view oneself as more important, more competent, and more prominent than others). When professional disagreements arise (and they frequently do as faculty monitor curriculum, promotion, and tenure and deal with resource issues), a good citizen will not take the arguments to a level of personal insult, abrasiveness, or hostility, nor resort to back stabbing, gossip, or involving students or community constituents in departmental disagreements.

So how do you prepare yourself to be a good citizen and establish your credentials early? A very useful type of activity is to serve as a student representative on departmental or college or university committees. Most institutions encourage student involvement in curriculum design and evaluation, and invite student participation in a variety of other roles (e.g., graduate student association, teaching award committees). Having been involved in at least one or two of these activities while in your doctoral program is evidence that you will be willing to do similar kinds of activities in the future.

The collegial aspects of good citizenship are a bit more difficult and challenging for some job candidates to handle, yet are exceedingly important (Harrison, Sowers-Hoag, & Gerdes, 1991; Harrison, Sowers-Hoag, & Postley, 1989). You should be aware that, from the minute you enter your doctoral program, you are being evaluated by faculty and administrators. You are being educated not only in the classroom, lab, or studio but also in offices, meetings, social gatherings, and any other event where both faculty and students are present. Even in situations where only you and clerical staff interact, you are being evaluated. If you are rude or demanding of staff, this behavior will usually be noted to the faculty or administrators.

Many faculty (and staff) talk among themselves about student progress and problems. Your reputation, whether good or poor, will both precede and follow you. These assessments of your academic and social skills will form the basis for later job references. Some future job candidates overlook the fact that references are often acquired both formally, via the student reference list, and informally, via inter-actions at professional conferences or phone conversations. You should pay attention to your interaction with other students, faculty, admin-istrators, and staff throughout the duration of your graduate work. If you have difficulty in the area of social interaction, we strongly recommend locating good faculty role models and mentors and, in extreme cases, professional counseling. Social skills can be improved, and, if you act early enough in the course of doctoral study, damage control is possible.

PREPARATION THROUGH NETWORKING

The last area in which you should begin to prepare yourself early in your program is that of networking. Get to know as many of the faculty in your department as possible. This includes not just persons with whom you will work most closely, but others outside your area of interest. This serves to broaden your exposure to the faculty, and increases the likelihood that additional job references and wider professional networks will be available to you when you go on the job market. The importance of networking in the education community is discussed in more detail in Chapter 4, "Your Search and Preparing Your Portfolio."

SUMMARY

As a prospective faculty candidate, you should consider a number of factors in preparing for the academic market. Entering the job market with the "PhD in hand" will certainly increase your marketability. To establish a solid track record, you should begin preparing your cre-dentials as early as possible in your graduate work. First, assess your interests, talents, and career goals, and continue to assess them through-out your studies. Next, give special consideration to preparation in the areas of teaching, publication, and presentation of your research and creative activities. Establish yourself as a good citizen by serving your department or other academic or professional organizations, and show yourself to be a good colleague to both faculty and staff. Finally, begin the development of professional networks to serve you when you begin your job search in earnest.

3

MATCHING YOUR CREDENTIALS AND PREFERENCES TO THE JOB MARKET

Finding the Right Fit

Issues related to faculty hiring and retention in higher education have received increased attention in the literature (Feld, 1988; Gibbs & Locke, 1989; Harrison et al., 1989). But an area that has not received much attention concerns the overall "goodness of fit" between the needs of academic institutions and the preferences and qualities of applicants on the academic job market. Nonetheless, it is important to understand the academic job market in your area and how well your own preferences and qualities fit with the market demands. So, before you begin your job search, you will need to think about what kind of job you want. Whether in a tight job market or in a high-demand market, thinking through some specific issues and weighing the importance of relevant factors will help you in your job search.

ACADEMIC JOB OPPORTUNITIES
IN YOUR DISCIPLINE

It is important to know what the job market is like in your discipline and how your credentials and qualities match current opportunities in the field. Current and anticipated shortages have been reported in fields such as communication, computer science, social work, business, and mathematics (Chesebro, 1991; Chronister & Truesdell, 1991; Harrison et al., 1991), whereas other disciplines such as English and psychology (Klesges et al., 1982) remain highly competitive. Despite the overall projected faculty shortages due to the graying of the professoriate and increased college enrollments, hiring standards and requirements are higher than ever before. Many institutions may elect to use salary dollars for other purposes or to defer their search for another year if an outstanding or suitable candidate is not found (refer to Chapter 1, "What Colleges and Universities Look For in New Faculty"). The successful job seekers prepare themselves well and present their personal and professional qualities in the best light possible.

Your first step is to investigate the hiring opportunities in your academic discipline. Ask for advice and information from your faculty adviser, department chair, or academic dean. You may also wish to speak with someone in your discipline who has just completed the job search and has acquired an academic position. Begin perusing the *Chronicle of Higher Education* for job announcements in your discipline, and note the qualities and characteristics desired in the announcements. Make a list of the most frequently cited qualities and characteristics and compare them with your assets. Ask your faculty adviser or department chair to give you names of people with whom you can speak candidly. You will want to find out how plentiful the jobs are and in what specific substantive areas or types of programs (large vs. small, undergraduate only vs. combined programs, teaching colleges vs. research institutions). For instance, a new approach or technique developed in your area may influence a high demand for faculty experts in that approach. Other changes may also affect the job market, such as the influence of managed care on the medical and health care fields. Ask for an assessment of characteristics and qualities most valued by the hiring institutions and what you should realistically expect to find on the job market. If possible, attempt to expose yourself to these valued areas and get some experience when applicable. If teaching experience is highly valued and you have none, then teaching at any level, even as an assistant, will be helpful. If publications are highly rated, then clearly you should be prepared to submit several manuscripts from your dissertation or research to scholarly journals. Many schools are now looking for faculty experienced in the use of distance learning technology. If that is the case, read about distance learning, visit a distance learning lab, and familiarize yourself with it as much as possible. Do everything you can to give yourself that extra added advantage.

You must be prepared for what to expect when you enter the job market. Advertisements may give some indication of what a department is looking for, but often these are only minimal standards that do not delineate the characteristics that would give an applicant a competitive edge. For instance, many advertisements may state that the institution will consider an ABD (all but dissertation) applicant. An applicant with the doctorate in hand will most probably be the more desirable applicant, however. In Chapter 4, "Your Search and Preparing Your Portfolio," we provide guidelines for the best ways to conduct your job search.

PERSONAL CONSIDERATIONS IN DECIDING WHERE TO APPLY

It is important to be aware of your own personal idiosyncratic considerations in your job search. A thorough and systematic job search can be extremely time-consuming and energy draining. You do not want to be spending your time (or the employing institution's time and money) on job opportunities that you know are not well suited for you. For instance, if you know that you despise cold wintry weather, do not apply for a position in Michigan. If you are easily bored in a small town, focus your search on schools in larger cities and urban areas. Small colleges are often isolated, and faculty are often required to live in the small town. The informality and potential closeness of such arrangements may be inviting, especially for young families. In geographically isolated areas, however, it may be difficult for a partner or spouse to find employment at the college or in the community. Smaller towns also tend to be more limiting in their access to recreation, entertainment, and cultural events. If these are important, look for areas where cultural or recreation outlets are close by. Make sure you investigate the area by contacting the area chamber of commerce and asking questions of persons who live in the area.

Remaining close to aging parents or support for children are all important considerations to be discussed before you begin your search. If you are fluent in a second language or interested in a new cultural experience, you may want to expand your search outside of the United States. We all have special considerations; now is the time for you (and your partner or family, if appropriate) to discuss and delineate the characteristics you want and those you do not want. Make a list and keep the list handy for ready reference.

INSTITUTIONAL CHARACTERISTICS
YOU SHOULD CONSIDER

Institutions of higher learning can vary widely. Consider those characteristics with which you believe you will be most comfortable and identify those that would be unacceptable or undesirable. For instance, large research institutions tend to have a heavy emphasis on research and scholarly publications, whereas smaller liberal arts colleges usually place a higher value on teaching and mentoring. Some schools may have a distinctive institutional personality, such as institutions with a strong religious affiliation, a women's college, or a predominantly minority institution. Some may place a high value on faculty involvement in the life of the school, whereas others do not. Smaller departments or academic units may have heavy committee assignment expectations, whereas larger schools have enough faculty to even out the burden. You will also find that some schools (particularly private schools, but not exclusively so) are entrepreneurial and will expect you to begin establishing external funding relationships, whereas others (perhaps public institutions) may have no such expectation. You should explore whether you want to be in an academic unit where others share your interests or views, or whether you prefer being on a faculty with diverse perspectives. Whether you think you would like to teach at the undergraduate or graduate level (or both), whether you prefer a highly democratic department to a hierarchical, more autocratic unit, or whether you want to teach small classes in the daytime on a traditional campus or large lecture classes perhaps on weekends or at nights at an urban campus are all legitimate issues for you to consider. Might you prefer being a big fish in a small pond or a small fish in a big pond? Is salary more important than being at an ivy league school? Is it important for you to have other junior faculty to relate to and collaborate with, or do you want a first-class senior scholar on the faculty to work under? Do you feel most comfortable when others like you are on the faculty (by gender, ethnicity, or race), or are you perfectly comfortable blazing a new trail?

The type of institution influences the academic purpose, institutional culture, and climate (Peterson & White, 1992). Doctorate-granting institutions consider the quality of an applicant's research to be more important than the quality of the applicant's teaching (Chesebro, 1991; Mooney, 1990). At the junior and community college level, as well as at small 4-year institutions, teaching quality is a very important factor when hiring new entry-level professors. For reappointment, promotion, and tenure, classroom teaching is evaluated with thoroughness and rigor. Student course evaluations are given a high priority in assessing faculty, and classroom visitations by deans or chairpersons are regular and perfunctory (Schuman, 1995). The teaching load at a smaller college is likely to be heavier than that at a research university, usually requiring faculty to teach three or four courses per semester, with a greater emphasis on college and community service. The breadth of teaching requirements at a smaller institution may also be greater, with a few number of faculty sharing responsibility for the curriculum.

In smaller colleges and departments, the institution is more likely to shape the social and general intellectual lives of the academics. In these smaller settings, where faculty tend to devote longer periods of their academic lives, deeper friendships are made among faculty, and more interesting and gratifying intellectual relationships are made across departments and other divisional barriers (Schuman, 1995). There is also a pronounced difference between the kinds of relationships that develop between teachers and students at small institutions. At larger schools, a faculty member may develop a close, mentoring relationship with a few strong undergraduate majors, but most likely will develop closer relationships with graduate students. In a small college, because the teaching loads are heavier and of greater breadth, and faculty are more deeply involved in student activities, faculty are more likely to develop closer relationships with many students (Schuman, 1995).

What stage of development is the institution and academic unit in? Some institutions may be in a state of reorganization. Although this is a potentially exciting time, it is possible that the academic unit you are in may be moved to a new college or school, or that you may have a new leader as the head of your academic unit. Are you willing to accept an offer without knowing where you will be housed or who your boss will be? Are you in a profession or discipline such as law, social work, or education that has a certification or accreditation process? If so, you will want to check on the state of the certification or accreditation. Make sure to ask when the program was last accredited and when it will be up for renewal. Application for recertification or reaccreditation can be a lengthy and intensive process requiring the commitment of all faculty. As a tenure-earning junior faculty person on a time clock, this may add strain to your workload. If the faculty are currently undergoing a major revision of the curriculum, you should ask for a time table of the revision and how this task and changes may affect you if you join the faculty.

The literature suggests that preferences among job applicants are quite varied. Most job candidates are searching for an academic position that reflects their own areas of expertise and interest (Barbezat, 1992; Sowers-Hoag et al., 1989). Across gender lines, it appears that male job candidates value salary and benefits as their most important consideration. Women applicants tend to place a higher value on student quality, teaching load, and social interaction within the department (Tolbert & Oberfield, 1991). Women also assign much more importance to the type of teaching assignments (Barbezat, 1992). Applicants belonging to a racial or ethnic group tend to look for institutions that are supportive to minorities. Minority candidates concerned about these issues should ask about the ratio of minority faculty within each school and department, how many minorities are hired on tenure earning lines, and if faculty mentors are available to provide assistance and support to the new hires. Candidates should also inquire about the retention and exit rates of faculty and the structures the institution has in place to support diversity.

SUPPORTS YOU WILL NEED TO BE SUCCESSFUL IN THE POSITION

Academic supports such as library resources, computer resources, specialized equipment, travel money, laboratories, research assistants, and the availability of workload reductions are only some of the factors that you may want to consider. Some academic units such as physical therapy require that students be trained on state-of-the-art equipment. Other academic units may need specialized equipment to allow you to continue with your research. Something as small as the lack of a sufficient library or library staff capacity may stall your progress. Do not assume that all institutions provide the same supports as your home institution—or that they do things in the same way. You must assess your needs and categorize them as absolutely essential, helpful but not necessary, and not important. If an institution requires a high level of research but cannot provide you with the laboratory or computer equipment necessary in your field of research, you should strongly consider an institution that can. Inquire as to whether teaching and research assistants are available only to senior faculty on grants or whether a junior faculty member can be assigned an assistant or receive a teaching load reduction to prepare a grant submission or conduct research. Do not assume that because you see state-of-the-art computer equipment in some faculty offices that you too will be the recipient of the same. Be clear in your own mind what you are willing to contribute and what you think you will need from the institution to be successful. If you are not clear on how things work or the amount of resources available for support, ask questions until you are clear.

MATCHING YOUR CHARACTERISTICS TO THE INSTITUTION

So much time and preparation goes into the search that you will want to do everything you can to ensure a good match. This is particularly true for tenure earning faculty positions that come with some sense of job security. The employing institution invests a great deal of time and resources in the search process, and is intent on finding a good match for the position. Over the next several years, after the initial hiring, the institution will invest further dollars and resources into the position. In most cases, it is not to anyone's advantage when a bad match is made and a position or job candidate does not work out. Therefore, it is extremely important that you be realistic in evaluating the type of institution where you will be able and willing to do what is necessary to attain tenure.

Sharing your thoughts and asking for feedback from your faculty adviser or department chair can be very useful. Ask for candid assessment and advice and be prepared to hear what they have to say without becoming defensive. Assuming that they have worked with you and become familiar with your style and abilities, their guidance in helping you sort out the most comfortable, productive, and successful placement can be enormously helpful. At the same time, you must keep your own preferences in mind. For instance, although your adviser may find you to be a very talented researcher and scholar, you may recognize this aptitude but also realize that you dislike the drudgery and tediousness of the research process. Under these circumstances, you may have an excellent chance at a position at a major research institution, but accepting such a position would mean dedicating yourself to years of work you dislike. If you work best with formalized structures, then you may be more successful at a college that provides research review groups, writing groups, and formalized mentoring. Or, if you know you are self-motivated and enjoy working alone, you may find these types of structures bothersome and a waste of your time. Although you may not find a perfect match, it is important that you consider elements that will help to ensure a good fit between you and the academic unit. What your dissertation chair or faculty adviser may want for you may be more a reflection of his or her own desires than your own. Having one's student placed at a prestigious institution or successfully engaged in research attracting national attention is a reflection of one's own accomplishments as a senior faculty mentoring young scholars. Be careful that you do not get caught up in the excitement or "honor" and lose sight of those things that will provide you with the best fit.

Many academic units have long histories, entrenched ways of doing things, and strong personalities that will change little after your arrival. Do not suppose that you can change the environment, personality, or values of the department when you arrive. Weigh what you perceive as the advantages and disadvantages very carefully. Follow your own instincts with respect to your comfort level, while keeping your professional goals clearly in mind.

SUMMARY

The prospective faculty candidate can use several strategies to maximize the likelihood of a good fit between one's own preferences and qualities and the needs and characteristics of the institution. Candidates should assess the job market in their discipline to ascertain the most highly valued qualities and characteristics sought by employing institutions. Where appropriate, candidates should prepare themselves to be able to meet the market demands and expectations, while also considering their own personal and professional goals.

4

YOUR SEARCH
AND PREPARING
YOUR PORTFOLIO

The academic job market varies across disciplines. In some disciplines such as English and foreign languages, academic positions are scarce and the competition is intense (Showalter, 1985), whereas other disciplines such as social work (Harrison & Sowers-Hoag, 1992) and computer sciences have more openings nationally than available applicants to fill them. Despite this variability, the graying of the professoriate discussed in Chapter 1, "What Colleges and Universities Look For in New Faculty," has provided a window of opportunity in most disciplines for a larger number of academic position openings over the next 10 years. For disciplines with many openings nationally, a good applicant can realistically expect to obtain a job within a year. In the disciplines where positions are scarcer, many applicants do not find a job the first year. If you prepare well, start the search process early, and continue to apply and interview for jobs even after you have been turned down, you will have a good chance at obtaining at least one acceptable job offer.

THE TWO-WAY STREET

As mentioned in Chapter 1, "What Colleges and Universities Look For in New Faculty," the job hunt is a two-way street. Academic disciplines are searching to fill a position vacancy; you are looking for a vacant place to fill. Both of you are very serious about the search. The search process allows both you and the academy an opportunity to screen each other to determine the appropriateness of fit. It may be difficult sometimes to maintain this perspective as you undergo the trials of the job hunt.

THE FORMAL AND INFORMAL SEARCH PROCESS

Immersed in your own search process, you may not be aware of the importance of the process and outcome from the institution's perspective. Because your relationship with the department may last for many years, faculty and administrators searching for tenure earning faculty are usually keenly aware of how their hiring decisions may affect their academic unit and academic life, both formally and informally. This is particularly true for smaller academic units. Although the hiring of temporary full-time faculty (e.g., to fill a sabbatical leave position) usually does not entail the same serious discussions and negotiations, the recruitment and hiring of tenure earning faculty can be as work intensive and emotionally charged for the people within the hiring institution as it is for you. Before you ever see an advertisement for an academic opening, faculty and administrators have invested a great deal of time and thought in the establishment of the position and the recruitment process (Lawhon & Ennis, 1995). Although the hiring process differs from institution to institution, there are some basic similarities.

In most cases, an academic unit will be given official permission from higher administration within the institution to recruit for the faculty position (Lawhon & Ennis, 1995). Smaller institutions and undergraduate-only programs seem to rely on informal contacts or local searches, whereas larger institutions offering graduate programs tend to use more formal national search methods (Sowers-Hoag et al., 1989). In larger academic units, a search committee will be established to provide leadership in the overall recruitment, interviewing, and selection process. In smaller units, all faculty may play important roles in the search and hiring process.

Once approval has been given to hire new faculty, the formal and informal searches begin. A search committee (if not already in existence) is appointed or elected, a job or position description is made, and advertisements are placed in several professional venues (e.g., the *Chronicle of Higher Education,* disciplinary newsletters or journals, minority publications, letters, and e-mail or Web page announcements to other departments and programs nationwide). The extent and thoroughness of this formal search process often depend on the size of the department or program and the available budget. Some departments will, by choice or necessity, conduct only local or regional searches.

In addition to the formal search, informal activities are used to identify key prospects and to build a solid applicant pool. These include contacting personal networks, alumni employed at other institutions, prominent senior faculty, and professional special interest group members. These contacts are often made not only by search committee members but also by academic administrators (deans, program directors, department chairs) and other faculty. When you are identified as a candidate by this informal process, you frequently enter the search "loop" with a built-in edge over candidates who have not been so identified. This edge may or may not even out during the next phases of the search.

Although this informal process may be helpful to institutions in identifying you as a potential job candidate, it may also result in your being overlooked if you are not a part of the search committee's network of contacts. It is hard to become part of the network at this point in the job search if you have never been part of the loop before. If you are a woman or from an ethnic minority that is underrepresented in certain disciplines, or if you do not make your job search known to your faculty, you may not be identified by this network process. Normally, your name would be put forward by faculty because they know your work, because they like and respect you, or because they know you are on the job market. Faculty might also put your name forward because they feel that you will reflect well not only on them personally but also on your home institution. Frequently, applicants who do not meet these criteria are left to fend for themselves in the academic job market.

THE TIMING OF YOUR SEARCH

Unfortunately, the best time for you to search for a position may not coincide with the traditional academic search calendar. Most academic positions (especially tenure earning positions) are advertised during the fall for positions to be filled in the following fall. Some positions are advertised to be filled as soon as possible or for a winter or spring term. Initial or informal interviews may be held at professional conferences, with most invited on-campus interviews taking place from February to June. If possible, try to time your search with the traditional academic calendar to maximize your opportunities. Although you may peruse job openings throughout the year, in keeping with a traditional academic calendar, you should seriously begin searching in late summer and begin applying for positions in early fall or as they appear. To avoid building up unrealistic hopes on your part, and unnecessarily taking up scarce time from the search committee, apply only for positions for which you meet at least most (more than half) of the criteria, and, most preferably, in your area of expertise (Sudzina, 1991).

SEARCH METHODS

Your most important challenge in the job hunt is to search out and pinpoint where the jobs are. This process is very important, and a challenge that you should embrace with committed devotion. No matter how well qualified or talented you are, you must uncover the job leads to pursue them. Another less talented applicant may get that prized academic position that you only recently learned about simply because he or she got there ahead of you. In the academic job market, the early bird really does get the worm. Many institutions publish firm application closing dates. Because advertising can be expensive, some institutions may place their ad for only a short period of time. Reopening a search can be expensive and time consuming, as well as risky for institutions unwilling to risk losing acceptable candidates already available in an applicant pool. Consequently, you must be continually diligent (at least once a week) and thorough in your search lest you risk losing out on some outstanding opportunities.

We discuss several methods that you can use to assist in your search for academic positions. These include networking and making presentations at conferences, searching the academic and professional printed publications, conducting an electronic search, and using your academic and professional contacts as brokers. Use a combination of all the methods available to you.

As discussed in Chapter 3, "Matching Your Credentials and Preferences to the Job Market: Finding the Right Fit," by the time you have reached the point of actively searching for a position, you should already have assessed your credentials and assets and matched them to specific opportunities in the job market. Keep a list of these, as well as your other professional and personal preferences, next to you while you are searching for the academic positions you may be interested in pursuing. Cross-referencing your credentials and preferences with advertisements will help keep you focused so that you can direct your energies most productively. If, however, you notice an advertisement that is particularly intriguing (perhaps it is in an exotic location or has a faculty member you want to work with), go ahead and make note of it. Some of the best and most productive matches have happened serendipitously!

The Traditional Search

The traditional job search includes recruitment ads, direct applications, and all the other avenues to employment we have come to expect. Most academic departments begin the search by preparing and placing an advertisement in professional newspapers or journals read by job seekers in their discipline. Almost all instructor and assistant professor positions across the disciplines are advertised this way (Burke, 1988). Many of these advertisements can be found in discipline-specific journals or in professional and scholarly association publications such as *Modern Language Association Job Information List* for English and foreign language disciplines or the National Association of Social Workers' quarterly newspaper, the *NASW News*. There are also some major generic listings commonly used by all disciplines, including the *Chronicle of Higher Education* and *Black Issues in Higher Education*. The *Chronicle of Higher Education* is the national newspaper of higher education and lists teaching positions across the United States as well as some international academic positions. Job listings in the *Chronicle* can be found in the "Bulletin Board" in the middle section of the paper. Jobs are listed alphabetically by job title and indexed by subject at the beginning of the section. *Black Issues in Higher Education* is a fairly new publication, published bimonthly, that is aimed at African American and other minority academics. It typically has an extensive job listing section. The journal published by the American Association for the Advancement of Science, titled *Science,* is a major outlet for postings in the biological and physical science disciplines. Most university and college libraries and career planning offices subscribe to these publications and make them readily available to job seekers.

The Electronic Search

The technological revolution is reinventing ways that people and jobs meet. Because of today's technology, resumes zap across cities or countries by telephone lines, large databases of resumes match people to jobs, help wanted ads flash on home computer screens and CD-ROMs, and videoconferencing is used for interviewing.

The Internet, the global network of networks, has become a powerful employment medium. The Internet represents an impressive empowerment for the job seeker. Classified help wanted ads and other employment information often are transmitted over online information services. Most commercial online information services have full Internet access. Much more in the way of job resources is available on the full Internet. Your local library should have a copy of the *Gale Directory of Databases, Volume 1,* an excellent reference listing complete online information services available. In addition, you can find online jobs on the Internet or on electronic job bulletin boards. The ads are usually generated by companies specializing in electronic job ads, government agencies, professional societies or trade associations, and ad hoc organizations operating as a public service. Most services displaying electronic help wanted ads deal with a wide assortment of occupations in a given field. You may need to be a member of a professional society or trade organization before you can use its job bulletin board, however.

It is expected that the Internet will be increasingly used by institutions to advertise for academic positions. If you do not yet know how to "point and click" and "surf the Net," it will be well worth your while to learn how. Resource sites on the Internet provide information on faculty positions as well as research, administration, and executive positions in academia. The following list represents some of the most useful sites for locating academic positions.

- **Academe This Week**
  (http://chronicle.merit.edu/.ads.links.html):
  This is the online version of the *Chronicle of Higher Education.* This is one of the most organized and easy to use resources on the Internet. On average, 1,000 or more faculty positions are listed in various fields. Unfortunately, only the current issue is available online. You should search this site weekly for appropriate position openings.

- **The Academic Position Network**
  (gopher://wcni.cis.umn.edu:11111/):
  The University of Minnesota's Academic Position Network provides notice of national and international academic position announcements. As with Academe This Week, the academic institution pays a fee to post announcements on this site. Unlike Academe this Week, however, this site continues to post an announcement until the position is filled.

- The Riley Guide—Employment Opportunities and
Job Resources on the Internet
(http://www.jobtrac.com/jobguide/):
The Riley Guide is a comprehensive list of various types of job positions, including positions in academia. The Riley Guide is often referred to as "the grandmother of resources for job seekers." Many academic institutions are not yet familiar with this resource, however, and continue to rely on Academe This Week and the Academic Position Network. As electronic posting becomes increasingly popular, this resource will become an even more useful tool.

- American Colleges and Universities Listing
(http://www.clas.ufl.edu/CLAS/american-universities.html):
This site is a list of all American colleges and universities. In addition to job postings, it offers information about the institution to which you are considering applying.

- Job sites at colleges and universities: Many colleges and universities have their own job postings on the Internet. The organization, timeliness, and scope of the postings differ with each academic institution. Within the next few years, the number of academic institutions posting positions electronically will increase, as will the quality of the organization of the postings. If you know that you are interested in certain geographic locations, you might locate specific geographic areas, academic institutions within those areas, and bulletin boards or job listings.

Networking

Networking, the cultivation of large numbers of one-to-one contacts, is also an extremely valuable method to assist you in your job search. Word-of-mouth brokering and networking by the right people can be a powerful tool in locating positions and opening previously closed doors. Over time, you will develop your own network of contacts and will ask them to serve as brokers in networking on your behalf. When you are ready to enter the job market, you should write or call your professional and academic contacts, letting them know of your intent to look for an academic position and asking for their help in identifying potential positions.

If you are a recent doctoral graduate or are close to finishing your doctoral program, your network of useful contacts may seem small. To extend your network, begin attending professional and academic conferences well before you are ready to enter the job market. Conferences are very good places to meet and get to know your professional colleagues.

Presenting scholarly papers is an excellent way to meet others in your area of specialization or who are interested in the kind of scholarly work you are doing. These people can become valuable contacts willing to introduce you to their circle of contacts. Whether you are a presenter or are simply attending the conference, make a concerted effort to meet and socialize with others while you are there. This may require that you ask others to join you for lunch or dinner. You will find that many persons will be pleased to be asked and grateful for the company. When you attend paper presentations or workshops, make a point of introducing yourself to the presenter and sharing your interests and work. Be complimentary of the presenter's work, and ask for citations or copies for subsequent reading. Most presenters are appreciative that someone expressed interest in their work. Many of these conversations and encounters result in useful collaborations on projects and the exchange of valuable information and contacts.

Do not overlook the potential of using the network from your own institution. The chair and members of your dissertation committee should be informed as to your position interests. The dean and department chair can also be valuable assets to you in your search process. Ask them directly for advice and to broker for you when appropriate. If you are interested in a specific academic institution, find someone in your institution who is an alumnus or has close contacts there.

Alumni who have graduated from your program before you who are now strategically placed in an academic unit that interests you may prove useful in your hunt. Prior graduates tend to remain loyal to their alma maters, and are often willing to intercede to assist others in being considered for a particular position. Many mentors and colleagues can be counted on to help you.

THE JOB APPLICATION

Once you have identified some academic position openings that interest you, you will need to be prepared to respond to the position announcements. Application materials vary across disciplines and fields. Although you will usually be asked to send a cover letter, curriculum vitae, and letters of recommendations (Showalter, 1985), you should read each advertisement carefully for instructions, because these may vary slightly. One advertisement may request the names and addresses of three references, whereas another may require actual letters of recommendation from three references. You certainly want to communicate to the search committee that you are capable of reading, understanding, and following directions. If your application is incomplete or inaccurate, it will probably be tossed aside with only a cursory review due to its failure to meet the minimal requests for the application package.

Some advertisements are not specific and may ask for a "dossier" or ask you to send your "credentials." These general terms do not provide enough specific information for you to respond. Either call the institution for more specific information or ask associates in your academic department or field for the standards for application in your discipline.

You may also be asked to supply a transcript, examples of your scholarly writing, or evidence of your teaching experiences, such as syllabi and course outlines. Get your application materials in order as soon as possible and add to your materials as your experience and productivity increase. Needless to say, all materials should be professionally finished and perfectly prepared. Typos, bad copies, inaccurate letters, and sloppy materials will land you in the institution's "not interested at all" category. Certainly, all work is expected to be word processed and sharply presented. A typed or sloppy curriculum vitae will be quickly tossed aside with comments regarding the applicant's need to enter the computer age. Remember, written or electronic application materials are often the only initial source of information for the search committee to consider in the selection process. This first impression is extremely important in your winning an opportunity to move to the next step in the application process. The following provides an overview of typically required application materials, and some tips on preparation to help you put your best foot forward.

The Cover Letter

Be prepared to send an individualized, unique cover letter to each department to which you are making an application. Many applicants use a basic word processed format and then tailor the content to the specific school. This is a good idea; however, you need to be attentive to making appropriate changes for the new application. We have seen application packets with cover letters addressed to the correct institution but containing the name of the dean of the last place the applicant applied. In another instance, an applicant addressed the cover letter to the correct person and institution, but within the body of the letter wrote glowingly of how he would like to join the faculty at the school's greatest rival. Mistakes such as these can be fatal to your job hunt, but you can avoid them by carefully proofreading your letters.

It is crucial to identify your address and phone number clearly on the cover letter. Obviously, if the search committee cannot reach you, it cannot interview you, and many reviewers will not take time to dig for this information. A search committee may be reviewing 100 or more applications, and so members generally do not have time to probe through materials (Wilbur, 1993). You may also wish to include a fax number and e-mail address if you have one. If you are in the process of moving, be certain to make note of this, specifying the dates and new location where you can be reached. Whatever information you decide to include, provide it in such a way that the employing institution will be able to contact you relatively easily.

Your cover letter should be fairly short (generally no more than two pages) and provide sufficient information for the reviewer to become interested enough to continue on to your vitae and letters of recommendation (McDowell, 1987). You must convince the reviewer somehow in this relatively short space that your application is worth continued study. Use simple, direct language indicating some of your knowledge of the institution and department and how you see your expertise and qualifications fitting with the program as well as the position advertised. You should specifically note the advertised position for which you are applying, highlighting your qualifications that correspond to the position. Document your expertise in the area, and demonstrate your experience by giving examples of some of the related work (research, teaching, etc.) that you have done (Reed, 1995; Sudzina, 1991). A cover letter can also be a good place to drop a name, if you can do it tactfully. Mentioning a mentor or professor of national reputation who is willing to validate your abilities can provide an important competitive edge.

The Curriculum Vitae

The curriculum vitae (also called a *CV, vita,* or *resume*) is a factual outline of your life as a scholar. As a beginning academic, you may feel that your curriculum vitae is too brief or not impressive enough. Rest assured that your vita will change in the future as your productive academic life progresses. For now, you must design your vita so that it is clear and neat and so that your strongest qualifications stand out. Organize your materials carefully so that reviewers can be clear about your credentials, experience, dates of degrees received, and dates and titles of previous employment. Ask several colleagues and your faculty adviser or department chair to provide you with some good examples of curriculum vitae in your field or discipline. This will give you some basis on which to build your own. Ask several trusted colleagues, faculty advisers, and perhaps your department chair to review your vita for you and give you feedback on both its content and its presentation style. Proofread your vita over and over again and then . . . once more. Any typographical or spelling errors can cause you to be dropped from consideration for the position.

Because the appearance of your application materials is extremely important, you need to assure yourself that your vita is both clear and neat. Otherwise, it will likely be tossed aside. To help yourself in this, you might want to consider using software to produce your resume. This will give you greater flexibility in tailoring your document, and will allow you to produce a quality vita at a fairly low cost. Although you do not have to have a computer program to produce a quality vita, you may want to visit a computer software store and explore what some of the computer-friendly resume writing software packages have to offer.

Regardless of whether you use a specially designed software package or not, your vita should be word processed—even if you have to pay someone to do it. Nowadays, you should learn a common word processing program and prepare these materials yourself. It will save time and frustration in the long run not to be dependent on others to do these tasks for you. A word processing program will allow you to consider several formats of presentation and make changes easily. Use a laser printer for the original copy of your vita. It is far better to produce multiple copies on bond paper than to rely on photocopiers.

The acceptable length of a curriculum vitae varies across disciplines and is dependent on productivity and length of time in academia. A good curriculum vitae is one that can easily be skimmed within a few seconds and yet has enough supporting detail to stand up under a careful and thorough review. You should organize the first page of your vita so that it contains the information about your greatest assets for the position. A vita that is not easy to skim or spot read may get short shrift among a stack of applications. Use highlighting and spacing to allow your curriculum vitae to be easily sight read so that important words that best convey your qualifications and credentials jump off the page.

All the information on your vita should be relatively straightforward. Reviewers should not have to struggle to understand it, and generally they will not take the time to attempt to calculate or guess at information. Do not in any way misrepresent yourself or your credentials on your vita (Harrison et al., 1989). If a block of time is missing from your professional experience, for instance, it is best to address the issue in your cover letter rather than to omit dates or other data from your vita. Experienced reviewers can easily detect vitae designed to obfuscate or hedge on information.

Your curriculum vitae should contain the following content areas: your name, current address, telephone number, fax number (if appropriate), and e-mail address (if appropriate), as well as a permanent address and phone number if you expect to be moving; information about your education; professional and work experience; research productivity; teaching experience; community activities; professional memberships; foreign languages; and any special honors or awards you have received. These categories usually appear in the same order on your curriculum vitae as presented here. Within each of these categories, the information should be presented in reverse chronological order, from most recent backward.

Name, Address(es), and Phone Number(s)

Your name, address, and phone number should appear prominently at the top of the first page. Your name should also appear at the top of every page. Include both your home and office numbers if available, as well as any fax numbers or e-mail addresses that you frequently use. If you do not have an answering machine, it is a good idea to invest in one for the duration of the search process. Relying on others to convey messages is not a good idea. An answering machine allows you to retrieve your messages fairly reliably, plus it allows you to access messages pertinent to your search while you are out of town.

Education

Within this section, you should list educational work in detail from most recent backward. This should include the institution, degree, specialization or field of concentration, and date when each degree was received. For example:

Education

Institution	Department	Degree	Date
University of Michigan	Psychology	PhD	1996

   Dissertation: "The Influence of Stress on the Dually Diagnosed"
   Dissertation Chair: Professor M. de Sade

Institution	Department	Degree	Date
University of Georgia	Social Work	MSW	1987
Barry University	Psychology	BA	1984

Awards
Predoctoral Fellowships: NIMH Research Fellow Award, 1994-1996

If you have not completed your degree, you should provide information regarding your latest stage of graduate work. For example:

Institution	Department	Degree	Date
University of Michigan	Sociology	PhD	in process

(Doctoral Candidate, May 1998. Expected Date of Completion, June 1999)

You should always include the title of your dissertation and the name of your dissertation chair. You may also list areas of specialization, additional areas of concentration, or your involvement in other research projects.

Experience

You should include all relevant experience in this section. For each position you have held, you should include the name of the institution at which you were employed, your position title, your responsibilities and accomplishments, and the dates of employment. Depending on the extent of your experience, you may wish to include separate subsections with division titles of "Professional Employment Experience," "Research Experience," "Teaching Experience," and "Volunteer Experience." Practice fields such as medicine, social work, and physical therapy may include a subdivision titled "Internship Experience." Provide a brief description of each item detailing the most interesting or impressive aspects of your position. Use verb phrases stressing what you accomplished and uniquely contributed. For example:

Teaching Experience

Position	Department	Institution	Date
Teaching Fellow	Psychology	University of Michigan	1997-1998

* Taught courses in human behavior, psychopharmacology
* Lectured and provided skill-based seminars on methods of counseling children and adolescents
* Writing across the curriculum, Fellow. Worked with students in critical thinking and writing skills

Publications and Presentations

Publications and scholarly presentations at national, regional, or even local conferences are of extreme importance for an academic position. They are generally listed in the standard bibliographic form for your discipline. This information should be listed by providing the most prestigious accomplishments first, beginning with the most recent within that category, followed by others in descending order. Always list each author by name, including yourself. Do not use et al. For example:

Referred Journal Articles
Smith, K. C. (1997). Promoting the spirit of American Indian women. (1997). *Journal of Women and Ethnicity, 15,* 154-163.
Jones, A. B., & Smith, K. C. (1997). Culturally relevant interventions with American Indians. *Research on Ethnic Practice, 9,* 90-103.

Professional Presentations
Smith, K. C. (1997, May). *The intersection between two cultures.* Paper presented at the 22nd Annual Conference of the National Association of Ethnic Practitioners, Sioux City, IA.
Jones, A. B., & Smith, K. C. (1997, June). *Re-establishing cultural identity among estranged groups.* Presented at the 45th Annual Program Meeting of the Southeast Regional Association of Cultural Anthropology.

Grants

If you have received funding, it should be listed here. This usually pertains to grants written by you, and may include grants on which you participated. You should make clear the degree of your involvement in writing and securing funding, as well as any role you played in the work the grant supported. You should list the dollar amounts for major funded research projects in this section as well. Funding received to support your dissertation or a fellowship is usually listed under "Honors." For example:

Co-Investigator, *Evaluation of a Substance Abuse Program for Women.* October 1994 to October 1997. Principal Investigator: M. de Sade. NIDA Small Grant Award ($27,000).

Scholarly or Professional
Memberships and Leadership

In this section, you should list your memberships in scholarly or professional organizations. Many academic disciplines and professions feel very strongly about membership in a national organization. Membership in professional organizations shows your commitment to your profession and your awareness of its activities (Showalter, 1985). For instance, a vita that does not indicate that the applicant is a member of *the* national professional organization for that field may not be considered as seriously as those of others that do list membership, especially if the applicant's qualifications are equal or less than the others. Consult your faculty adviser or departmental chair regarding the importance of belonging to specific organizations within your field. If you are still a student, you may wish to join those organizations now because most provide a reduced membership rate for students.

If you have been particularly active in some organizations or in university committee work, you may also include it here. For example:

Member, National Association of Community Psychologists
Chair, Planning Committee, Southeast Regional Association of Minority Psychologists
Member, American Association of University Women

Additional Information

This is an optional section that may be used to list any special competencies or miscellaneous information you think may be important. For instance, competency in a foreign language, with special laboratory equipment, or in a special field should be noted in this section. Usually, information about personal factors such as hobbies, religious affiliation, marital status, and children is omitted on resumes. If you are disabled or a military veteran, however, it is appropriate to note such factors according to personal preference.

References

You may include a list of people who have agreed to write letters of recommendation for you. If you have a wide range of expertise or experience relevant to the position, try to include a broad range of references, each of whom can address various aspects of your experience. Although this category is optional, if any of your references are of national prominence, it can be helpful to have their name listed on your vita. Extra consideration is often given to applicants who have worked under or are recommended by outstanding scholars or professionals. Identify each reference's institution and provide phone numbers. Select persons who know you well and know your work. Always make certain in advance that these persons are willing to serve as a reference for you and will provide a positive recommendation for you.

If the advertisement requests that applicants provide letters of recommendation, then it will be your responsibility to contact your references and make certain that your recommendation letters have been sent and have arrived at the institution. First, call your references to ask them to submit letters of recommendation for you. Follow up with a written reminder reiterating the position, institution, and address. Then follow up again to be sure the letters have been received at the department to which you are applying. Good references tend to be busy people—provide them with sufficient information and gentle prompting.

■ Other Requested
   Materials

It is common for an advertisement for a position in the academy to request samples of your writing, scholarly work, or research. You will need to have at least one paper worthy of being mailed out along with your application (Shetty, 1995). You may use manuscripts submitted for publication or articles already in print, parts (or all) of your dissertation, and papers or projects prepared during your doctoral education. As with all other application materials, these should be reproduced in good quality.

THE PAPER SCREENING

Once you have been identified by either formal or informal means, have applied for the positions in which you have interest, and have sent each institution your cover letter, vita, and references, the institutions will conduct "paper" screenings, in which the search committees review your application materials. From the search committee's perspective, ideal candidates are those whose credentials and record of accomplishments most closely match those that the institution is seeking. Depending on the size of the applicant pool (and mission of the department or college), certain credentials, such as degree in hand (versus having completed all but dissertation, or ABD), teaching areas, or research and publication record, can serve as immediate screen-in or screen-out criteria. At a minimum, you must meet the qualifications stated in the job announcement.

Next, you will be placed into one of three categories on the basis of the paper screening: in (worth pursuing), out (not worth our time), and maybe (if the in-candidates fall through, and those about whom search committee members have additional questions).

Other than meeting the minimum qualifications for the position, what kinds of considerations or judgments are made by the search committee to categorize you and the other applicants? The ideal candidate is one who represents a perfect fit between what the school or department needs and what the candidate offers. Obviously, each individual search committee member will make some independent judgments about your degree of fit, and will assess factors such as where you did your graduate work, which faculty you studied with, teaching or research experience, narrowness of specialty areas, and range of teaching or research interests. The committee will also judge the overall visual and substantive presentation of your application materials. Often, individual judgments made by search committee members will be discussed and rehashed with the committee, and collective decisions will be made about the relative attractiveness of the different candidates.

Many academic departments are actively recruiting and trying to hire underrepresented populations (usually ethnic minorities and women) in their disciplines. In these instances, when two or more applicants have similar credentials, preference may be given to the ethnic minority or women candidates. Affirmative action often places ethnic minority candidates at a distinct advantage in the current job market. Unfortunately, this advantage has led some nonminority candidates to resent the whole process, to believe that nonqualified candidates are hired, or to resign themselves to the idea that their top choices for academic employment are probably out of their reach because of affirmative action hiring. This may not be a real concern. [1]

Dr. Peters' Selection Process

Dr. Peters was called on to chair the search committee at Ivytown College, which must fill a vacancy in the mathematics department. An old friend of his who had gone through graduate school with him just called him and told him about a young woman, Ruth W., who was finishing up her doctorate and looking for a position. She recommended Ruth highly, and Dr. Peters asked that Ruth send her curriculum vitae, promising to look at it closely.

About a week later, Ruth's curriculum vitae arrived. Dr. Peters had received 52 other applications during the week, and because his classes were currently going through mid-terms and he had to correct and grade 60 papers over the weekend, he didn't really have time to look closely at any of them. He noticed, however, that Ruth's cover letter and other materials were spotless, and appeared to have been professionally printed. As he glanced at Ruth's materials, he noticed that she had highlighted the fact that she was interested in teaching calculus, having already taught that course three times to undergraduates during her doctoral studies, and had highlighted that she had acted as an adviser to graduate students during that same time period. This information caught Dr. Peters' eye because these were important qualifications the search committee was looking for, that is, teaching experience and close student contact. Dr. Peters placed Ruth's vita on the top of the pile of other applications for closer review later.

At the search committee meeting the next day, the applications were passed around to the other committee members. They each glanced through the materials quickly, and then started discussing the ones they felt most interested in. Dr. Peters mentioned that Ruth had been recommended by his friend, and that he felt her application materials showed some promise. After a quick perusal by the other committee members, Ruth's vita was placed in the pile scheduled for telephone interview along with 10 others.

Dr. Peters called Ruth the next day. He spoke with her for about 20 minutes, asking her if she was still interested in the position. He was impressed with how polite Ruth was, and how calm she seemed to be during what he realized was probably a fairly stressful interview. He discovered that she was a single mother who seemed to deal with the rigors of child rearing with a sense of humor. When asked if she would need assistance in finding child care for her daughter if she were hired at the college, Ruth responded that she would appreciate the assistance, but that it would not be essential because she had handled the problem before. She reported that she had put together a neighborhood child care center with the help of several other single mothers in her neighborhood who had similar problems. Dr. Peters was very impressed with Ruth's creativity and her willingness to work in the community. Two weeks later, he called again and asked Ruth to come to a brief interview at the national conference scheduled for the following month in Chicago. Ruth agreed, and a time was set.

Ruth arrived at the appointed time, but had to wait about 30 minutes for the committee to complete an interview with another candidate who had been late arriving. The search committee members noted that this delay had not ruffled Ruth. Later, they also commented on Ruth's apparent preparation for the interview, noting her thoughtful and complete answers to their questions. They were particularly impressed by her questions at the end of the interview, when she asked how they might see her fitting into the school's community involvement with the local hospital. No other candidate had indicated any knowledge of this project that the school had become involved with in the past several years. Ruth had clearly done her homework.

After Dr. Peters and the other search committee members returned to their school, they met to discuss who should be asked to the campus. Ruth was the first of three possible choices. She accepted the invitation to the campus with obvious enthusiasm. Dr. Peters asked her if she had applied anywhere else, and she replied that she had applied at numerous places and had even gotten two job offers. She admitted that she had put them off until after this interview because she was so interested in the possibilities there. Dr. Peters appreciated her honesty, and reported it to the other committee members, putting them on notice that they were clearly going to have to impress Ruth as much as she was going to have to impress them.

It was a long day for Ruth when she came for the on-campus interview, having arrived at 9:00 in the morning after a 4-hour flight, and then being escorted around the campus in the pouring rain. She maintained her sense of humor, however, and was polite and gracious to everyone. She had arranged ahead of time for one of the faculty members to provide her with a computer for her colloquium presentation, but the rain had held that person up, and no one knew how to find the equipment. Although Ruth was disappointed, she simply asked for an overhead projector, and went on without a fuss. Later, faculty discussed among themselves how this might be an indication of how she would handle the multitude of crises that inevitably assail faculty during the school year.

Faculty noted among themselves that they liked Ruth personally. Even those who shared none of her academic interests admitted that she was invariably polite, and made an effort to find out about their lives and interests. It was clear to several of the faculty that she would probably be an excellent colleague, perhaps even a friend as time went by. After interviewing the other two candidates, Dr. Peters and the other committee members recommended to the administration that an offer be made to Ruth. Negotiations went smoothly, and Ruth was hired for the fall.

SUMMARY

In this chapter, we looked at what you need to do to prepare yourself and your portfolio for your job search. A successful search process requires commitment and hard work. You should use not only traditional recruitment ads found in discipline-specific journals and newspapers; consider using the Internet and academic and professional networking to identify appropriate job openings. Your cover letter and curriculum vitae must be presented so that they can be easily and quickly read by the search committee, but they also must contain adequate information about your qualifications and experience to impress the committee enough to pursue you. Your material must be both attractive and substantive so that your job application will pass the committee's paper screening. The next phase of the job search, the interview, is discussed in the next chapter.

NOTE

1. We should make two points about minority hiring and affirmative action. First, there is the maxim and principle that in the event of two similar, equally qualified candidates, the edge should go to the minority candidate; this is especially true in disciplines and departments where ethnic minorities and women are underrepresented. Second, in most fields, the number of minority candidates desired by academic institutions far exceeds the actual number of minority applicants available (Chesebro, 1991; Morgan, 1993). Combined with the faculty shortage issue, in general, there are plenty of academic jobs to go around. In the field of social work, for example, for one academic year, we estimated the number of open faculty positions to be approximately 400 nationwide, most of these at the assistant professor level. For the same academic year, there were approximately 100 new doctoral graduates.

5

APPLYING FOR AND
GETTING THE POSITION

A completed application is an implicit statement that you are ready to interview on short notice (Wilbur, 1993). Before you are even contacted, a fairly rigorous screening process has already taken place. If the employing institution contacts you and expresses interest, you can expect that your application has been reviewed at least by a screening committee of the department, and perhaps by the department chair or dean. It also may have been reviewed by the entire faculty and upper administration. Some departments prioritize candidates into a short list of three to five of the top candidates and a longer list of acceptable but not top candidates. Applicants on the short list are generally contacted first.

It is not uncommon for departments to contact your references and their own informal contacts who may know you to assess others' opinions of you before contacting you. Make sure your references know where you have placed your applications and for what types of positions so they will be prepared if a department calls them. As mentioned in Chapter 4, "Your Search and Preparing Your Portfolio," obtain prior approval to list someone as a reference. Never take chances: Be certain that your references are prepared and willing to give you a positive recommendation. A mediocre or wishy-washy letter can at best raise a red flag, and at worst be the kiss of death for your job search.

THE TELEPHONE SCREEN

After completing the paper screening and contacting your references, the department may conduct a telephone interview with you. The telephone interview allows departments to conduct a brief interview at low cost. The purpose is to screen out any candidates on the short list who are no longer interested in the position, are unable to respond well to questioning, or appear inappropriate for the position despite an attractive curriculum vitae. Some institutions do not use this first telephone contact as an interview, but instead set up a brief face-to-face interview. In either case, this will be your first personal contact with the screening committee other than through your application materials, and at no other time during the hiring process are first impressions more important than during this brief screening interview.

At this point in the search process, the screening committee is assessing the extent of your interest in the position, your ability to substantiate your skills and expertise verbally as outlined on your vita, and, to some extent, your social and communication skills. The telephone screening can be a particular challenge for some applicants. Here you cannot rely on facial expressions, eye contact, or personal appearance to help you communicate. Highly qualified candidates have been known to fall flat and eliminate themselves through nervousness or some other innocent interview faux pas.

When an interested institution calls, you should convey obvious pleasure at hearing from the department, and maintain a level of interest and enthusiasm throughout the conversation. Because this interview is so important, you might want to practice your phone interviewing skills with a colleague, friend, or mentor. Even if questions are posed differently by the interviewer, you will find that practice will aid you in providing smooth, well-thought-out responses. Tape-record your responses and ask for feedback from the person role-playing the interviewer. Ask a mentor or senior faculty person to help you construct questions that you can expect to be asked during the initial phone screen. You should be prepared to discuss your past and current research, future research interests, teaching experiences, and interests, as well as substantive issues in your discipline and specific area of expertise. In addition, you should be prepared to respond to more general questions such as your interest in the department and institution and your attraction to that area of the country. Think through your responses to these hypothetical inquiries carefully, and ask for feedback on your responses. Practice your responses until you feel confident in their content as well as your phone interview style.

If you have applied for several academic positions, keep a reference log by your phone listing the individual institutions and the specific positions for which you have applied. This ready reference should also contain names of key people in the department and any special information about the department or school. Be prepared to show that you have done your homework and are somewhat knowledgeable about the institution and department.

THE COMPUTERIZED JOB INTERVIEW

Since 1978, more than 6 million job applicants have been interviewed by computer. At this time, the majority of the users of this type of system are in the private corporate sector, which hires large numbers of people. A consensus among users points to an overall improvement in the quality of the employee hired because the computer helps decision makers overcome problems inherent in the traditional job interview. These problems include factors among interviewers and the consistency of questions (Kennedy & Morrow, 1995). Advocates of computer interviewing suggest that computerized multiple choice questions are structured to require thoughtful reflection, and are programmed to spot inconsistent or problematic answers. Because people tend to respond more honestly to a computer than to a human interviewer—especially in sensitive subject areas—if you find yourself in the position of being interviewed by computer, you should be careful not to reveal anything to the computer that you would not reveal to a human interviewer. The next step in computer-assisted interviewing will be interactive video, which will draw insights into how a job applicant would react to certain situations. Currently, computer-assisted interviewing is rarely used by institutions of higher learning to screen faculty candidates. Given its growing popularity in the corporate world and its use and efficiency, however, it will probably become a tool valued by the academy before long.

INTERACTIVE VIDEOCONFERENCING

New interactive videoconferencing technology permits interviews across town or across the country. This new technology allows the employing institution to interview a larger pool of applicants because the applicants do not have to undergo the expense of going to the institution unless it is fairly sure that they are strong candidates. SEACnet (Southeastern Atlantic Coast Career Network) is a consortium of 22 public and private university career centers. Using videoconferencing technology, SEACnet connects employers with prospective job applicants. If you are a student at one of the consortium institutions, you can enter your vita in the electronic database and search the system for job openings. Employers post position vacancies and can request vitae that meet the position's hiring criteria. Employers can schedule a videoconferencing interview at a university in the consortium. Employers and applicants can see and hear each other, as well as view a vita, online. Either party can transmit or receive data. Although videoconferencing seems to be advantageous from the institution's point of view, it can be a trying experience for the candidate.

Rather than undergoing a face-to-face interview, you are interviewed
with the new and perhaps unfamiliar technology of the cyberspace
interview. Do not assume that the same interviewing techniques used
successfully in a face-to-face interview will be successful in a cyberspace interview. Some mannerisms that are appropriate face to face
can be misinterpreted in the cyberspace interview because the context
is different. Videoconferencing will probably not replace face-to-face
interviews totally. It may gain popularity as an initial screening tool,
however.

THE FACE-TO-FACE BRIEF INTERVIEW

Not all academic disciplines conduct telephone screening interviews,
and not many use computer or videoconferencing methods, but most
do conduct some type of brief, face-to-face screen interview with
candidates prior to inviting a candidate to an on-campus interview.
These brief screenings usually take place at professional conferences
or meetings that candidates and faculty are already scheduled to
attend, thereby saving the university the cost of campus interviews for
candidates who might be screened out following the brief interview.
These brief interviews are also valuable to you, because you can screen
out institutions that obviously do not meet your needs.

Where Do Interviews Take Place?

Brief face-to-face screenings usually take place at professional
conferences or meetings that candidates and faculty are already scheduled to attend, thereby saving the university money. Generally, they
take place in less formal venues than offices, such as over a meal,
coffee, or cocktails; in a hotel lobby; or in a hotel room. One or more
members of the search committee, other faculty, or an academic
administrator may be present. In a relatively brief time frame, say 1
to 2 hours, the interviewers will attempt to assess the degree of fit
between you and the department, your ability to substantiate the skills

and expertise outlined on your vita as they relate to the job position, your level of social skills, and your physical presentation style.

▓ Who Can You Expect to Be at the Interview?

Some brief interviews may be conducted by only one interviewer, whereas others may have a fairly large group of faculty present for the interview. It is not uncommon for several interviews to be scheduled back-to-back on the same day, with some time in between each interview for a critique of the candidate before moving on to the next applicant. Do not be surprised to find a candidate being interviewed while you are waiting for your appointment. If you are scheduled later in the day, you may find that the interviews are running late. This is not unusual, and should not alarm you. Just make sure that you are on time for your appointment. If the interview is scheduled for a location you are not familiar with, scout it out ahead of time to ensure your timely arrival.

▓ How Should You Look and Act?

We cannot stress enough the importance of your appearance, demeanor, and interview style. Some faculty will begin to size you up quickly based on their first impression. These first impressions are often difficult to change. Dress professionally. Despite the relative informality of the conference or traditional faculty attire, men should be in a suit or, at the very least, a coat and tie. Women applicants should wear a fairly conservative suit or appropriate dress. Many applicants can share horror stories of last-minute spills, tears in stockings, or wet clothing from luggage left in the rain by a careless porter. Dress for the interview early enough to repair any possible damage.

Do not drink alcohol or smoke cigarettes during the interview, even if they are offered to you. Should the interview take place during a meal, order a moderately priced menu item that can be consumed with relatively little difficulty while interacting (stay away from spaghetti, thick submarine sandwiches, and other foods that tend to splash, drop, or require extensive chewing). Now is the time to remember all that your parents taught you—your dining manners and etiquette will be judged as surely as your qualifications and credentials.

▓ What Kinds of Questions Will They Ask?

To substantiate the skills and expertise outlined in your vita, you may have to answer tough, challenging questions put forth by the interviewers in a face-to-face interview. Regardless of your discipline or area, if you present yourself as an expert on a certain topic or methodology, the interviewers will want (and will try quickly) to establish that you are in fact an expert in that area. Unfortunately, in areas where there are legitimate philosophical or methodological differences, some of your answers may prove to be the "wrong" ones in the eyes of the interviewers, even though these views may more accurately be described as different from the interviewers' biases. As with the telephone interviews, you should compile a list of potential questions, practice your responses, and ask a trusted colleague or mentor to critique your responses and provide you with feedback. Videotaping one or more role-played interviews can allow you to critique your nonverbal as well as verbal communication.

In addition to practicing before a video camera, you can improve your interviewing skills by using a computer to coach you with verbal responses. Currently on the market are computerized self-tutors that help you become skilled at job interviewing. The software (most quite modestly priced) uses artificial intelligence to challenge your answers. Based on the knowledge of interviewing experts, the software is programmed to continue questioning the applicant prompted by individual responses in different creative ways. The software will critique your responses. For instance, it may suggest that you return to a certain question and improve the substance of your answer. Suppose you said that you desire a position at X University because the school is geographically convenient. The software would suggest that you add to your answer. You might then respond with a statement about the outstanding reputation of the university or the quality of the faculty in xyz academic department. The computer continues to critique your responses and provide prompts until you have given an

acceptable answer to the question. Subsequent sessions pose alternative questions.

In addition to questions about your research and areas of expertise, you might be asked about your career goals, your plans over the
next 5 to 10 years, your educational philosophy (Dewey & Gardner,
1983), and your approach to classroom teaching. Be prepared to
discuss your dissertation, your planned research agenda for the next
few years, and, if relevant to the institution, any ideas or plans you
may have for external funding. Theoretical perspectives, empirical
approaches, and philosophical debates within your discipline may also
be points of discussion.

How Should You Address Inappropriate Questions?

State and federal laws protecting your privacy and individual
rights forbid employers from asking questions that can lead to dis-
crimination on the basis of race, sex, religion, national origin, or
physical disability (Klingner & Nalbandian, 1985). Just because some
questions are potentially illegal does not mean that they are no longer
asked. Questions regarding your marital status, plans for having
children, or provisions for child care are often asked. Questions about
your spouse's employment status or about your age (perhaps referring
to your extensive years of experience) are also inappropriate. Certainly there are times when such questions are asked innocently, either
out of interest or in an attempt to assist you in finding a position for
your spouse or good child care or to introduce you to others with
similar interests. You must use your best judgment in responding to
these types of questions. Highlight your strengths without necessarily
answering the question. If you feel uncomfortable with something
being asked, you may ask the interviewer to clarify for you how the
question relates to the position you are seeking.

What Else Are They Looking For?

Despite the scholarly focus of the interview, it is important that
you remember that the interviewers are looking for candidates who
can relate easily to other colleagues and students, are self-confident

without being arrogant, are comfortable and pleasant in interpersonal situations, are not overly nervous or caustic, and might be someone with whom the faculty member may want to have an occasional lunch. Particularly in small departments or programs, faculty can spend a great deal of time with each other working in task groups, on committees, and in faculty meetings. Collegiality and an ability to work and play well with others are important characteristics to convey. Many faculty hires made at the assistant professor level end up are career-long commitments on the part of the faculty and the institution. If for no other reason than this possible 20- to 40-year relationship, existing faculty and administrators are looking for individuals who can be good colleagues. Once your objective credentials and qualifications are shown to be adequate, your level of social skills and your potential for collegiality become increasingly important. It is rare for a candidate's brilliance or potential as an outstanding scholar or scientist to override demanding and generally unpleasant behavior. Tolerance for such departmental "characters" has lessened, especially with new faculty hires. Many interviewers will view your ability to respond to tough questions and carry on an interesting discussion and conversation as indications of how well you will relate to students. During brief screening interviews, evidence of good social skills, including a sense of humor, can serve you well.

▓ How Important Is Your Presentation Style?

Related to social skills is what we call *physical presentation style,* a combination of physical appearance and personal mannerisms. Most faculty in U.S. colleges and universities like to think of themselves as our nation's intelligentsia, mostly liberal or at least open to human differences, and more or less immune to societal biases and prejudices. In fact, university environments are microcosms of the larger societal environment, and personal biases, prejudices, and mannerisms are rampant. If we think of appearance and mannerisms as existing on a continuum, then extremes on either end are probably the most problematic to many faculty. For example, if you are extremely well dressed, you may fit in as poorly as you would if you were extremely poorly dressed. Likewise, being extremely young or extremely old, extremely conservative in appearance or extremely liberal in appearance, and extremely overweight or extremely underweight all potentially make you a less attractive candidate. Extreme or unusual mannerisms, such as a very loud or unusual laugh, very rapid or slow speech, and obvious nervous gestures, are also potential strikes against you.

What difference to an individual's ability to teach and conduct research would any of these physical attributes make? Of course, mostly none is the answer. The reason they become problematic is that they draw attention to you, and often result in people around you becoming uncomfortable. Biases toward the safe middle ground, away from extremes, will rarely be articulated openly; if they are, they are usually described between colleagues, and in the context of how your teaching or research might be affected. Be forewarned that looks and actions can and do make a difference. If you are the only scholar or outstanding teacher in a pool, then some of these characteristics might be overlooked. On the other hand, if the pool is otherwise strong or there is at least one other candidate equally qualified, these kinds of attributes can eliminate you from consideration.

▓ How Should You End the Interview?

Often the last 10 to 15 minutes of the interview are left to provide the applicant with an opportunity to ask questions. Many applicants are not prepared for this opportunity and are often left uncomfortably searching for something to say. This may be a good time to demonstrate your familiarity with the institution, the department, and perhaps some of the publications of the faculty. This can be done very appropriately in the context of your acknowledgment of a desire to establish the degree of fit between you and the institution. Be prepared with some questions that communicate your desire to learn more about the department while determining how you could best fit in. At this point, you should probably stay away from any specific hiring questions such as salary and teaching load. You may ask for a sense of the timing for the search and when the committee will be moving to the next step in the process, however. At the end of the interview, be sure to shake hands with each member of the interview party, smile, and look at them while expressing your appreciation for the interview.

When you return home from the conference, you should send a brief
note to each member of the interviewing party to thank them and
reiterate your continued interest in the position.

THE ON-CAMPUS INTERVIEW

The on-campus interview is an extended version of the brief screening,
with two additional components: the colloquium or sample lec-
ture/presentation and the class seminar. By the time a department has
decided to invite three to five candidates for an on-campus interview,
it has probably determined that all the invited candidates are competent and acceptable for the position. Typically, candidates are given
very little notice of an invitation for an on-campus interview (Formo,
1995). As a result, you should have all your materials and presentations prepared well in advance. All costs of your trips for on-campus
interviews are eventually paid by the host school, but most schools do
not provide a cash advance to support your visit to the school. Instead,
you will be reimbursed by the school. This will require an initial outlay
of money for cabs, hotel, meals, and sometimes plane tickets. It may
take as long as 30 to 45 days for you to receive the reimbursement
(Iacono, 1981; Perlman, 1976). Be prepared to spend money when
job hunting! The on-campus interview may be the most critical aspect
in determining who will be offered an academic position (Klingner &
Nalbandian, 1985). The same kinds of criteria are used by faculty on
campus and the same individual and collective judgments are made
about candidates. During this period, the faculty continue to assess
your degree of fit with their department and its needs, your long-range
scholarly and collegial potential, and your tenurability. From the
moment you are picked up at the airport to the moment you are
dropped off at the airport, you are being assessed. You may meet with
students, some engaging faculty as well as some curmudgeons, a dean,
an academic provost, and outside persons in the community. Be
prepared to repeat yourself often answering similar questions asked
by a variety of different persons. Each response (no matter how often

you have had to repeat it) should be given with enthusiasm and interest. In addition to being interviewed by faculty and administrators, you will be interacting with departmental staff, including secretaries, work-study students, and perhaps graduate assistants. You should be as concerned about your interactions with the graduate assistant showing you the university computer facility and the secretary attempting to fill out your reimbursement papers as you are with faculty and administrators. Informal impressions garnered by staff and students can often have an influence on hiring decisions. Flexibility and a sense of humor will serve you well during the on-campus visit.

The on-campus visit could conceivably involve a presentation to faculty, a lecture to a class, a group interview, several individual meetings with faculty and higher administrators, some meals, and a reception (Gaus, Sledge, & Joels, 1983). Find out the interview schedule in advance, what meetings and events to expect and with whom, and what expectations will be made of you with respect to presentations and class seminars. Bring plenty of copies of your curriculum vitae (faculty are notorious for misplacing them and asking you for an extra copy), and any handouts or other materials you may need for your presentations. You may also want to bring extra copies of any of your research or published work. Do not pack any of these materials in luggage that will be checked with the airline. In fact, do not check anything important on the airplane. Bring all the essentials in carry-on luggage.

▧ The Colloquium

The importance of an excellent presentation cannot be overemphasized. A poorly prepared and poorly delivered presentation can rarely be overcome. The presentation is an opportunity to assess your research (generally the candidate will present his or her dissertation research), how you may present or perform in the classroom, how you respond to questions and how quickly you can think on your feet, whether you have a commanding presence that can sustain student interest as well as the interest of colleagues, and how flexible you are in stressful situations. Be prepared for some pointed and challenging questions—some of which may be posed simply to see how well you respond. If you do not know an answer, be confident enough to admit it. Remain calm and do not become defensive even in the face of criticism of your work or unreasonable questions. Consider using handouts and visual aids during your presentation to allow the audience to focus on something other than you occasionally, and to serve as presentation cues should you become nervous and forget your place in the presentation. If you are planning to use any high-tech equipment in your presentation, such as a computer-screen projection system, make certain ahead of time that the department can provide the space and other ancillary needs you may have. Just in case, bring plenty of old-fashioned back-up materials such as copies of handouts, slides, or transparencies. We have witnessed several presentations that were less than impressive because the candidate was not able to use the equipment (for whatever reason) to produce the visual aids. Practice your presentation, videotape it, and ask peers and mentors for feedback.

Faculty can be unpredictable, and almost all academic units have at least one faculty member who will be difficult during the presentation. Examples include the person who whispers loudly to a neighbor throughout the presentation or who frequently takes issue with your comments or rebuts your statements. Some candidates have told us of some particularly rude behavior during interviews. Practice in advance how you might respond to pointed, challenging, or unreasonable questions from the audience. Our overall impression is that most faculty are embarrassed by such behavior and hope that the candidate does not reject the whole institution as a result. In fact, most faculty are quite considerate. Having gone through the same interviewing process themselves, most are empathic, attentive, and interested in your presentation.

You may find yourself being videotaped—this is usually done to enable faculty who could not attend your seminar to view it. Courteous departments ask your permission in advance to tape your session, but do not be surprised if you are not asked. Do not make a fuss over this; just do a good job.

▓ The Classroom Seminar

Candidates are generally informed ahead of time if they are expected to teach a class or conduct a classroom seminar as part of the on-campus interview. To be safe, ask well before arriving for the interview. Generally, if a candidate is expected to teach a class, he or she is told the topic for the class, given options of topics to teach, or asked to select his or her own topic. Candidates should be prepared to use their best teaching skills and demonstrate several teaching strategies, including didactic and interactional methods. Communicating your enthusiasm for the topic being taught is critical. When possible, make plenty of eye contact with students and step outside from behind the lectern and toward students to communicate your interest. Piquing student interest and eliciting student input is likely to garner favorable student evaluations of your seminar.

▓ The Individual Interview

Candidates are usually scheduled for individual interviews with faculty, the department chair, the dean, and the academic provost. In some cases, each interview may be quite different; in others, several interviews may seem quite repetitious. Typically, faculty are most interested in your personal and professional fit with the academic unit. Their interests tend to be rather insular with respect to how you can contribute to the curricular offerings, research plans, and service needs of the unit. Administrators tend to have a wider scope, focusing on your fit with and potential contribution to the college or university, the greater community, and the overall enhancement of the visibility and reputation of the institution. Your potential for tenurability will be assessed at all levels. Be prepared to respond to questions across a wide spectrum from details about your dissertation research to how you see yourself contributing to the institution over the next 10 years.

Take advantage of the individual interviews to communicate your interest in the position and the institution. Make certain to point out at least one positive view you have gained since coming to visit (the lovely campus, the friendly faculty, the bright, enthusiastic students, or perhaps the impressive equipment). Ask questions during the interview that communicate that you also are assessing how well you fit with their vision and expectations.

▓ Social Events

Social events are usually part of the on-campus visit. They serve as an opportunity for faculty to observe you in a less formal setting. It is your opportunity to observe how faculty interact with each other and gain a sense of how well you fit with this group of individuals. These occasions generally allow you to talk about your work in a more comfortable environment, and allow you and faculty to interact informally and socially. You should feel free during this time to ask questions and get to know faculty. Show interest in their lives and work, in the workings of the department, and in the area in which the college or university is located. Some faculty may take this opportunity to try to pry some gossip or interesting tidbits from you about your home institution or specific faculty with whom you have worked. Do not attempt to endear yourself by sharing any negative or unpleasant information about others, and certainly do not confide any negative stories about your dissertation committee or doctoral experiences. No matter how tired you may be, you should remain positive and enthusiastic with each person you encounter throughout the social event.

▓ Assessing the On-Campus Visit

Take notes on your trip home about your feelings and experiences. Assess your level of professional and personal comfort with the faculty, the department, the administration, the university or college, and the geographic location. Make a list of remaining questions that you will want to be sure to ask later if you are contacted for a job offer. And of course, send a personal note of thanks to the person who arranged and hosted your visit. Be sure to file for reimbursement for your travel expenses. Courteous departments will see that this is explained to you prior to your departure.

THE INSTITUTION'S DECISION

Once the search committee and faculty have narrowed the list of top candidates down to one to three individuals, how will they decide who will get a job offer? More than likely, the academic administrator, such as the dean or department chair, will make that decision. He or she will base the decision on several considerations. First, who is the candidate that the faculty recommended or ranked highest? Second, which candidate is likely to bring the most prestige, research skills, or teaching range (depending on the size, type, and mission of the particular college or university)? Finally, and this consideration is often the sole concern of the administrator, which candidate is the easiest, the one who presents the fewest obstacles for the administrator? Examples of hiring obstacles include spouse or family issues; unreasonable salary, lab set-up, or teaching load requests; and job start delays ("Can I start in January instead of August?"). Although these obstacles can cause you trouble, when the pool is slim or there is clearly one outstanding candidate whom the university wants to hire, faculty and administrators will usually look for solutions aggressively.

The Story of Janice S.

Janice S. was a PhD student about to get her doctorate in political science, and planned to teach at some university or college as soon as she was able to find a job. She was particularly interested in a midsize institution, Sunnyside University. A professor she had known during her undergraduate work, Dr. Roberts, was now employed at Sunnyside, and Janice felt that she might be able to count on him to help her, although she had not seen him or spoken to him since her undergraduate work was completed. Although she had worked part time during her doctoral program, Janice's financial situation was not comfortable; indeed, she was worried that she would not be able to make her house payments if she didn't find employment soon. Feeling the financial pressure, and at the same time anxious to begin her career as a university professor, Janice decided to approach the university and express her interest in working there.

In the January before the national conference was to be held in March, Janice sent an e-mail message to Dr. Roberts stating that she was about to receive her doctorate and that she would like to interview at the university. Although he had had no contact with her since undergraduate school, he remembered her as a promising student, and suggested to the search committee that it take a look at her at the national conference.

Janice had never been to a national conference before and, because she was unfamiliar with the hotel in which the conference was being held, was about 10 minutes late to her interview. Because of her rush, she was even more nervous than she would ordinarily have been, and she felt that she had not shown herself off to best advantage as the interview closed. The committee was polite but not especially friendly. Although it was somewhat impressed with Janice's curriculum vitae and her personal presentation, with approximately 11 other candidates to interview, it did not want to commit to her in any way. Later in the evening, however, Janice came into the bar where the Sunnyside faculty were relaxing after the long series of interviews, and approached Dr. Roberts, asking him how he felt she had done in the interview. He stammered a noncommittal reply, and withdrew from her as quickly as he could without being rude, watching in dismay as she approached two other members of the committee with the same question.

When the search committee returned to the university, there were already messages to each member from Janice telling them how much she had enjoyed meeting with them and how she was looking forward to having an opportunity to come to the school for an on-campus visit. Later that week, she called Dr. Roberts and asked him if the committee was going to invite her to the school, again stating her great desire to work there. Dr. Roberts was unable to give her an answer because the committee, having been back only a few days, had not had the chance to meet and decide who it was going to ask.

Actually, Janice's interview at the conference had not gone as badly as she had feared. Her curriculum vitae had shown some good teaching experiences, and she had indicated that her area of specialization was what the faculty was looking for, Latin American politics. The committee decided to invite Janice and two other candidates for on-campus interviews.

When Janice arrived at Sunnyside University, she was scheduled for several individual interviews with faculty who had not had the opportunity to meet her at the conference. She handled these with calm assurance, and felt that she was fitting in well. Then Janice was faced with her colloquium. She was anxious about this, though she was actually quite well prepared. She gave a thorough explanation of her dissertation, complete with good visual aids backed up by colorful and artistic handouts. During the colloquium, one of the faculty asked her what her main area of interest was. She immediately stated that her great love was European economics. The members of the search committee glanced quickly at each other, remembering that this was not what she had said at the initial interview at the conference. They already had a professor well versed in European economics; they really needed someone who specialized in Latin American politics.

After the on-campus interview, Janice flew home. On the flight, she reviewed the process, and she had the feeling that it had not gone well. She therefore resolved to call the director of the school the following day to see if she could find out how the committee felt about her. The director was not pleased to get her call. There had been no opportunity for the committee to meet and discuss the visit, and indeed there were two other candidates to see before any decision would be made. He indicated as much to her, and firmly told her that the committee would let her know as soon as it was able.

The committee was not able to meet until late in the following week. In the meantime, Janice called three of the committee members "just to check in with them." When the committee finally met, there was some discussion about Janice's obvious qualifications, but faculty expressed concern about the discrepancy between her interest in Latin American politics as stated at the conference and her interest in European economics reported at the colloquium. And the director remembered the call the morning following Janice's on-campus interview. He remembered the desperation in her voice. The committee was clearly not convinced that Janice could fill its needs, and the director made the final decision not to make her an offer. He was afraid that her neediness would sap the energy of the entire department.

SUMMARY

In this chapter, we examined the interview process, emphasizing the critical importance of developing appropriate presentation and interviewing skills. We looked at the different skills needed for telephone, computer, and interactive videoconferencing, as well as face-to-face and on-campus interviews. We also discussed the on-campus presentation, the class seminar, and individual interviews. We attempted to provide some sense of how to prepare and what to expect. Assuming a solid educational preparation, diligence, hard work, and practice are the most important keys to success in opening the doors to the academy.

6

NEGOTIATING A
JOB OFFER

We have seen instances where faculty position candidates were so thrilled to have received an offer from a favored institution that they simply accepted the offer outright and forgot to inquire as to the details of the offer or to negotiate aspects of the offer. Never accept an offer outright—especially on the phone. Instead, you should immediately express your delight and enthusiasm while asking for some time to think through the offer. In fact, most department chairs and deans would be surprised to have you accept the offer immediately. In this chapter, we provide you with some advice on handling the interminable wait for an offer, how to negotiate and accept an offer, and how, appropriately and with grace, to reject an offer.

KEEPING YOUR SPIRITS UP AND
THE JOB HUNT ALIVE

After all your hard work in the search and interviewing process, you now find yourself sitting by the phone waiting for an offer. This may be a particularly difficult time. Don't just sit there! Continue your search—new positions are advertised continuously. Continue to apply for those that interest you. Contact all your references, colleagues, and advisors. Let them know about your campus visits and your more recent applications. Continue to express interest by writing letters to departments you are interested in (Iacono, 1981). Do not write or call so frequently that you become a nuisance or, worse, that you appear desperate. When you have completed an on-campus interview, send the department chair, chair of the search committee, and search committee members a personal note thanking them for the visit and their hospitality. If any one faculty member went out of his or her way for you or made a special effort to make you feel welcome, be sure and thank him or her as well. Do not ignore the potential influence of support staff in the decision-making process. Secretaries, work-study students, and graduate assistants often give informal input that may or may not have some influence on voting members. If an office manager or secretary was particularly helpful in setting up plane and hotel reservations, for instance, be sure and send him or her a thank you note as well.

If your peers are also in the academic job market, share information and search and interviewing tips with them. This may be a time of great anxiety for each of you. A doctoral cohort can provide much needed support and relief. As tough as it may be for you right now, celebrate with any of your peers who have received job offers and try to gain any knowledge you can from their experience. Remember, these peers with whom you may be feeling some sense of competition will very shortly be important colleagues and contacts within your academic network.

THANK GOODNESS . . . A JOB OFFER!

You have found the perfect academic position! They certainly seem very interested in you, and you are very interested in them. You have delivered a well-received presentation, your on-campus visit revealed no serious ghosts in any closets, no mean crotchety deans are prepared to bite your head off. In fact, you were enthralled with the campus, liked the departmental faculty, and love the geographic area. The faculty have all said that you would fill an important gap in the curriculum, they support and are interested in your research, and they seemed to enjoy your witticisms at lunch. This is all good. But remember . . . the search for an academic position is not over until the offer is accepted. Even when negotiating the terms of an offer, you may decide that the offer does not meet your needs or the institution may withdraw the offer. Job offers are unpredictable. You may have had a wonderful interview with a department, and it sends you a rejection letter. Financial cutbacks, sudden changes in priorities, legislative hiring freezes, and many other factors can influence the institution's ability to follow through on an advertised position. No matter how promising an offer may look, continue seriously with your job search until you have signed an official letter of offer.

You have been diligent in your search and carefully prepared for your interviews. No doubt within a few weeks of visiting several schools for on-campus interviews, you will receive a phone call offering you a job. Most offers are first made by telephone. The initial phone call is usually for the purpose of sounding out the likelihood of acceptance and to begin discussing some practical details. Always express pleasure at hearing from the school. Avoid making a commitment right away. Be honest about your situation and be reasonable.

BUT DO I HAVE TO GIVE
THEM MY ANSWER NOW?

There are competing desires between your wanting to find out what other offers you will receive and the school's desire to fill the position as soon as possible. You will want time to consider the offer and perhaps give time for other schools to contact you with an offer. The department wants to get its first choice, but very likely it also has a prioritized list of other acceptable candidates. The department must weigh the chance of losing other desirable candidates while waiting for your decision.

Most probably, the department will give you time to consider the offer and make a decision. Any time between a few days to 2 weeks is fairly common. Several weeks are not uncommon, although extensions beyond a month are fairly rare. You should feel comfortable asking the department how long it plans to give you to make your decision. Be sure to convey enthusiasm at the same time that you are requesting extra time to consider the offer. Again, remember that no offer is final until you receive it in writing. Although instances of withdrawn verbal offers are rare, there have been instances where candidates have become so aggressive, demanding, or unreasonable during the negotiations that the department has withdrawn its offer.

NEGOTIATING THE JOB OFFER

At this point, you have received at least one or two phone calls from the department—probably from the chairperson or the dean. The first call may have been preliminary to assess your continued interest in the position, to reassure you of their continued interest in you, or to begin initial discussions regarding the job offer. The second call is generally more definite and specific in nature, with at least a statement that you will be made an offer for the position. Usually, the second or third phone call will specify the details of the job offer. You can expect an average of 2 to 3 weeks to elapse between the on-campus visit and the first phone call indicating the possibility of a job offer (Minner, Ellsworth, & Prater, 1994).

Asking Questions and Clarifying Information

You should be prepared to ask questions when you receive the offer, or very soon after. We suggest that you make a list of questions as soon as you return from your on-campus visit—or better yet, compile your list on the plane ride home from the visit. If you have been invited to several on-campus visits, you may confuse issues or forget some critical questions pertaining to a specific school. Because you will have different questions for each institution you visit, you will need to make a separate list for each school. Having a list of questions readily available when the department calls is vitally important. It is not good to call the department over and over again to ask questions. You will appear disorganized, nit-picky, and greedy. Busy department chairs or deans do not have time to respond to your phone calls constantly no matter how badly they may wish to hire you. Avoid asking trivial questions, and focus on issues that are serious negotiating points for you. Remember to stay enthusiastic and pleasant in your discussions. You do not want the department chair or dean to regret the decision to offer you the position. In the next section, we provide suggestions for information that may be important, as well as negotiable points you may wish to discuss within the context of the job offer.

Some on-campus visits are extremely informative, whereas others yield little information about the general operating procedures of the department. If you have important questions about departmental functioning that are not necessarily related to the negotiation of the job offer, you should begin asking those questions after the department has clearly expressed interest in extending you an offer. Make it clear that these are points of interest and understanding, and not necessarily related to negotiating the offer. For instance, you may wish to ask for copies of the tenure and promotion criteria, personnel guidelines, curriculum syllabi, the by-laws of the department, and policies regarding support for conferences and paper presentations. There are other important details you will want to know as well. For instance, if the college or university has multiple campuses, make sure you know where your office will be located. You may want to find out how much cross-campus traveling will be expected of you. Are there any off-campus programs and, if so, will you be expected to teach off campus and how often?

If you are seeking a tenure earning position, it is critical that you ask specific questions about tenure and promotion to help you select a position that matches your goals and strengths (Duell, 1994). Policies regarding tenure and promotion generally appear in faculty handbooks and other written material. Request these materials and read them carefully. You will want to determine whether tenure and promotion are linked together ("up or out") and the time frames when probationary faculty will be considered for tenure. Be sure to inquire as to whether the institution has tenure quotas and what percentage of the faculty you will be joining is tenured. Questions regarding the relative weights given to teaching, research, and service in the tenure decision are also important, although the weights given to tenure criteria often change over time. Ask what supports are given to tenure earning faculty and if progress of junior faculty is reviewed before the actual time the tenure application is due (Duell, 1994).

■ What to Do When Your
    First Choice Isn't Your First Offer

Not all applicants get an offer from their first-choice institution. Some applicants do not get an offer for an academic position at all. Others get and accept offers for academic positions at their second- third- or last-choice institution. What should you do when you receive an offer from an institution that you find acceptable, but you have not yet heard from your first choice?

First, we suggest that you allow yourself a sigh of relief that you have an offer in hand and congratulate yourself for your accomplishment and good fortune. Next, you must decide if you wish to negotiate for a lengthier decision time to allow an offer from your first choice. You may simply ask for additional time, citing an upcoming on-campus interview or the need to discuss the offer with your family. Most academic units will not be willing to leave the position open for long, however. We suggest that you contact your first choice to let it know that you have been offered another position. Ask what its time frame is for making a decision. Generally, you can get some sense of the level of interest in you. If you are a top-ranked candidate, your first-choice institution will most likely inform you of this once it learns that you have a job offer. It may also ask you to allow a day or two to put together an offer to you. When you are pushed by the offering institution and you have no alternative offer from a more preferred institution, you will need to make your decision. If you are willing to take a risk, you may be able to buy a little more time by saying "if you need an immediate answer, then the answer is no." Obviously, under these circumstances, you risk the possibility of being left with no offers.

■ How to Negotiate the Job Offer

The actual job offer is written by the department, chair, head of the search committee, or dean. It is usually approved by the provost or chief academic officer of the college or university. Do not consider yourself hired until the offer has been negotiated and you have received and replied to a written offer. Negotiation begins after you have received the verbal offer and ends after you have signed and returned the written offer. This is the time that you are in the strongest position to ask for salary or other special conditions that may be important to you. First, it is important that you understand all the details behind the job offer before you accept. These questions can and should be posed in a manner that appears to reflect your excitement and enthusiasm about joining the department, rather than quibbling. For instance, it is perfectly appropriate to ask if the department knows yet where your office will be situated. This simple question alone is apt to prompt a discussion by the department chair about your office and its location and furnishings, as well as a notation about your faculty office neighbors. For a beginning junior faculty member, asking how large and well-appointed your office might be is not a good idea. You will want to know what course content the department is interested in your teaching, what kind of secretarial support is available, what kind of special support is available to support tenure earning faculty, and the like. These conditions and supports vary widely across academic units within the same institutions and across institutions of higher learning. Some academic units place a priority on resource use to support tenure earning faculty, whereas other academic units reserve support resources for the senior faculty. In some units, senior faculty are given first choice in course selections, whereas others assign courses according to expertise.

Final negotiating criteria usually include such things as salary, rank, terms of employment conditions, teaching load, class assignments, moving expenses, support to attend conferences for paper presentations and professional development, start-up money, and equipment (computer, laboratory, etc.; Burke, 1988). They may (rarely) also include a job offer for your partner or spouse (see Chapter 7, "Dual Career Issues"). Until lately, the academic job market has not been conducive to negotiation unless the applicant has been offered more than one job. As the academic job market becomes increasingly competitive, however, institutions may be more likely to negotiate. Currently, the room for negotiation is not great. You must clearly decide on negotiating issues that are important to you. Discuss these issues thoroughly with pertinent others (such as a potentially affected partner), and specify the issues on a list by priority for your reference during the negotiation. This is important because negotiating an offer can be extremely anxiety producing or uncomfortable. You do not want to forget your important negotiating issues or appear to be confused during the negotiation process. Remember to maintain a pleasant demeanor throughout the negotiation. Most important, do not rush into any agreements you will regret later.

Be prepared to assess the appropriateness of the salary initially offered to you by knowing the salary ranges for the type of position and institution. National salary studies are frequently published and available in college and university libraries. Institutions are generally aware of the national average in salaries by rank across disciplines, and how their offer compares. You will find that salary offers will vary, however. Smaller colleges and academic units tend to have less resources, although this is not always true. Larger institutions or institutions of higher learning in high-cost areas will generally reflect a slight to moderately higher difference in salary. Again, this is not always the case. Some highly prestigious institutions offer lower salaries to beginning faculty with the expectation that the job applicant will reap future benefit from association with the institution. For the most part, there is little latitude in salary negotiation for a junior faculty position. There tends to be more room for negotiation if you are being hired to strengthen a department or to expand its range of interests. Targeted minorities in high demand, an applicant with an unusual amount of postdoctoral experience, or a top-ranked applicant with a firm and higher offer from another school may be successful at negotiating a higher salary. If a department is unable to offer you a higher salary or there are other issues of more importance to you, the department may be willing to negotiate on other matters. In fact, if you are a highly desired applicant and the department is simply unable to offer you a higher salary, it may be inclined to offer some alternative resources. For a variety of reasons, one-shot resources may be more readily available to the department chair or dean than salary dollars that require an obvious ongoing commitment. These may include reduced teaching loads for the first year, computer or laboratory facilities, relocation expenses, summer research funding, initial start-up funds, research or teaching assistants, or specialized research equipment.

Try to discuss all your important negotiation issues in as few conversations and as early in the negotiation process as possible. Because the department chair or dean may need to take your requests to higher administration for approval, he or she will appreciate your parsimonious approach. Chairs or deans are not likely to appreciate a last-moment negotiation tactic or request after having spent time putting together what was thought to be an acceptable package. It is more likely that you will be successful in your negotiating if you are thorough, concise, straightforward, and pleasant during the process. Once you have signed and returned a written letter of offer, your bargaining leverage will significantly decline, and the chair or dean will most likely consider this phase of the search process closed.

Negotiating for Years Toward Tenure

Some institutions may consider granting an applicant some years of credit toward tenure upon appointment to the tenure earning position. This is relatively rare, however, unless the candidate has accrued time in a tenure earning position at another institution and has an outstanding teaching and research record. Even under these circumstances, the institution is not likely to grant the candidate the same number of years toward tenure. Negotiating for time toward tenure can have negative consequences despite an outstanding record. The move from one institution to another will most certainly cause a disruption in the candidate's productivity. Institutions usually assess the candidate's record before arriving at the institution and after joining the institution. Greater weight is generally given to the work accomplished while at the tenure granting institution. Should any unforeseen circumstances occur affecting productivity, the candidate will most probably still be required to adhere to the prenegotiated years earned toward tenure. The general wisdom in the academy is to err on the side of safety and, no matter how tempting, to forgo negotiating time toward tenure unless the applicant can ensure that productivity in teaching, research, and service will continue at the same or higher rate.

ACCEPTING AND REJECTING OFFERS

Think very carefully before deciding to accept a position. We suggest that you reread Chapter 3, "Matching Your Credentials and Preferences to the Job Market: Finding the Right Fit," as well as your personal and professional preferences list. For most recent hires in the academy, teaching load, academic reputation, quality of colleagues and students, and family needs are the most important factors influencing their position acceptance (Sowers-Hoag et al., 1989; Teevan, Pepper, & Pellizzari, 1992). Accepting an offer can provide an immediate relief for your current (un!)employment status, but an ill-made match can be devastating for you and the employing institution for years to come. Verbally accepting a position and subsequently rejecting the offer also can have serious long-term repercussions. In addition to costing another candidate a job, the academic unit may lose the position if it has been unable to fill the line. At best, it may be forced to leave the position vacant, expend more resources to readvertise the position the following year, and again incur the expenses of a search. Nonetheless, the institution will most probably not hold you to your initial acceptance because no faculty or administrator desires an unwilling person in the department. It is very possible that such an action on your part will result in negative consequences to your reputation, especially among educators in your discipline. The networks of discipline-specific educators are tight and active, and gossip often spreads quickly regarding such instances.

▓ Accepting a Position

If you have decided to accept a position offered verbally over the phone, immediately send a letter confirming your acceptance and outlining any pertinent details discussed in your phone conversation. Be sure to convey your delight at the prospect of joining the faculty and how you are looking forward to receiving the written letter of offer.

Upon receipt of the written letter of offer, read the details carefully and, if it is in agreement with your verbal discussions and negotiations, sign the letter and return it before the expiration date of the offer. You should immediately inform your advisers, references, the placement bureau, and other departments considering you for a position. Telephone all academic units where your candidacy is active and then follow up with a written letter withdrawing your application from the pool of candidates. Written letters of appreciation should be sent to advisers and references who were helpful to you in your job search.

▓ Rejecting a Job Offer

If you find yourself in the position of rejecting an offer, you are probably doing so because you have accepted another offer, you do not find the offer acceptable, or you are not interested in joining the institution making the offer. Despite your reasons for rejecting a position offer, always do so with graciousness and appreciation for the institution's interest in you. Be careful not to burn any bridges behind you. Thank the committee for the offer and interest in you. If you are accepting another position, let the institution know where you will be going. Consider sending a personal note of thanks to the department chair or any faculty who were particularly kind or helpful. You will most likely be meeting these people again at conferences and professional meetings. You may even be collaborating on research with some in the future or serving with them on national boards or committees.

Kevin's Choice

Kevin L. was very excited. He had received a call from First Choice University offering him a junior faculty position in the social work department. It had been a tough 4 weeks since his on-campus interview at FCU, and he had done a considerable amount of soul searching about his performance there, alternately thinking that he had done well and then feeling certain that he had ruined his chances by an off-hand remark he had made to one of the professors. He had succeeded in keeping himself from badgering the director of the department by immersing himself in looking for positions elsewhere, and indeed had gone on two other on-campus interviews, one at a college in his hometown in the Northwest and the other at a large university in Texas. He kept in touch with classmates about their job searches, and sent out curriculum vitae to several other institutions. He received an offer from the Texas school, but had put it off for 3 weeks because FCU had called him to make sure he was still interested in the position and let him know it still had two more candidates to see before finalizing the choice. He knew he would have to make a decision very soon, or lose the one offer he had received.

Although Kevin felt that the Texas position would be interesting, that school was a research-oriented school, and Kevin was interested in spending time in the classroom. It had clearly wanted him, offering to pay all his moving expenses and to furnish him with a new computer that would have helped him continue the research he had begun with his dissertation. He had requested and received copies of tenure and promotion criteria, and was impressed with the amount of support given for conferences and paper presentations. Kevin felt, however, that he fit best at FCU, and was hoping that it would accept him.

Kevin was not at home when the second call from FCU came. When he checked his answering machine his initial impulse was to grab the phone and shout "YES!!," but he instead got his enthusiasm under control before returning the call. When he spoke to the director, he expressed his delight at the possibility of coming to the school. Because he already knew what the Texas school was willing to do, Kevin had a complete list of questions to ask FCU by the phone so that he could compare the offers. Although he had called Texas three times to clarify its position, he had learned enough through that experience to know exactly what he needed to know from FCU.

Although he wanted very much to get the position at FCU, he was not willing to give away everything in the process. For example, because he lived in the Northwest and FCU was located in the Southeast, Kevin knew that his moving expenses would be very high. The Texas offer had had some real appeal because the school was willing to pay the entire amount. This is what Kevin's list of questions looked like after speaking with both schools:

	Texas	FCU
1) Salary?	$32,000	$30,000
2) Moving expenses?	All	None
3) Tenure		
a) Up or out?	Yes	No
b) % of faculty	50%	75%
c) supports	No review	1 review
d) weights		
4) Research	60%	20%
5) Teaching	30%	70%
6) Service	10%	10%
7) How many campuses?	2 (30 miles apart)	1
8) How often?	1X week	3X week
9) What courses?	Research I	Research I
	Research II	Practice II
	Elective of choice	

Kevin let the director at FCU know that he needed time to consider the offer and compare it to the one received from

Texas. The director was understanding, and suggested he call back in 3 days. After thinking it over on his own and talking with faculty in his doctoral program, Kevin decided that the difference in salary was not as important as the amount of teaching time he would be allowed, but he was still very concerned about the moving expenses. Therefore, he called the director at FCU and asked if the school would consider picking up his moving expenses because Texas had agreed to do so. The director explained that, because it was a smaller school, the budget couldn't accommodate that much, but offered to pay $1,500 of the moving costs and reduce the teaching load from three times a week to two times a week. Kevin expressed appreciation for the offer, and said he would let the director know his decision within the next 2 days. He went back to his faculty and discussed the alternatives, and finally decided to go with FCU's offer. He immediately contacted the director at the Texas university, thanked him for the offer, and told him of his decision to go to FCU due to his particular interest in teaching. He was gracious, and thanked the others on the faculty there who had supported him.

SUMMARY

The faculty candidate should continue to search for a position until a written and signed job offer has been secured. In this chapter, we have attempted to help you think through some of the issues associated with negotiating the job offer. Being prepared by knowing the essential points for negotiation from your perspective will provide clarity in your decision making and communicate your earnestness to the employing institution. Refrain from going "back to the well" frequently. Keep a list by the phone and be certain to cover all your needs in detail, most preferably in one (at most two) conversations.

Maintaining goodwill among colleagues is important in higher education circles. After you have accepted an offer, contact other schools where you have interviewed to let them know of your decision. Also contact your references and those who have been helpful to you. Each person should get a personal note of recognition and thanks from you.

7

DUAL CAREER ISSUES

If you are a faculty job candidate who is in a relationship, whether marital or cohabiting, in which your partner also pursues a career (academic or otherwise), you will likely face the additional burden of your partner needing to secure employment. The term *burden* is used intentionally because accomplishing the feat of both partners gaining employment is not always the easiest task. It is certainly possible, however (Harrison et al., 1991). In the current competitive job market, some colleges and universities seem to be more willing to negotiate, and some institutions are very aggressive in these efforts and sensitive to the needs and demands of dual career couples. Given the increasing age of marriage in the United States, it is not unusual for graduate students to meet their future mates while studying the same area or discipline in graduate school. Even couples who have had preexisting relationships prior to graduate school or are in different disciplines may face challenges in trying to locate two jobs, or challenges that are entirely novel (e.g., partner's job or business is site specific). In this chapter, we review some of the options that you should consider when seeking jobs when you have a partner. We also provide some insight from the perspective of the employing institutions.

COUPLE EMPLOYMENT
CONFIGURATIONS

Before exploring different options available to dual career couples, we should note that there are four basic configurations of couple employment status. Each of these configurations presents different difficulties depending on the demographics of the college or university to which you are applying and the kind of employment your partner is seeking.

In the first configuration, both partners are in the same academic field or discipline, with different areas of specialization. In the second, both partners are in the same academic field, with the same area of specialization. The third configuration is one in which you are an academic seeking faculty employment, and your partner is a nonacademic with an established career. The fourth configuration is one in which you are an academic seeking a faculty position, and your partner is a nonacademic with no specific career interests.

It is very difficult to speculate on which dual career configuration presents the fewest problems to finding employment for both partners. Your chances of finding academic or other employment in an area depend on the demographics of the location (e.g., size and population trends, other government, industry, or business), the number and size of academic institutions in the area, and the type of employment being sought by your partner. We explore some of the problems you will be facing and then look at possible solutions.

PROBLEMS ARISING FOR
DUAL ACADEMIC CAREER COUPLES

The probability of finding two academic positions at the same university in the same area of specialization (e.g., two Shakespeare experts) is extremely low. The probability of finding two positions within the same discipline but with different areas of specialization (e.g., two history graduates, one in the American Civil War, the other in Russian history) is higher, yet in most instances, this might be more difficult than finding positions in two different disciplines (e.g., chemistry and philosophy). Although you may be very lucky and find positions at an institution that fit you and your partner's qualifications and interests exactly, and both of you are equally desirable as faculty candidates, usually one or the other of you is more attractive to the department regardless of discipline or field. In this case, the department that wants one of you the most (i.e., the best fit) usually becomes the advocate for the other.

You must understand first of all that the degree of effort that the university will be willing to expend on finding placement for your partner may depend on how much it wants to hire you. You and your partner should not, however, interpret a university's or college's lack of job offer, or apparent unwillingness to secure a position for your partner, as an indicator of your worth or competence. Many confident and competent faculty candidates think that if the university wanted to hire them enough, the institution would figure out some way of making the hiring situation with their partner work. This is not always the case, because resources, interdepartmental relationships, and faculty responses usually play a large role in whether or not such deals can be worked out.

If the college or university suggests that you handle this problem yourself, however, it might be telling you that this particular institution (or department) is not very interested in you, and is neither dual career nor gender sensitive. At this point, you and your partner should decide if you want to pursue positions at an institution that is either not seriously interested in you or is not sensitive to the needs of its faculty. Of course, depending on the job market, you may not have a choice.

You need to be aware that pushing for the institution to find a place for your partner can backfire. Let's look at the problems that a search committee may face in trying to find a position for your partner. If you and your partner are in the same field, the department that is interested in hiring you may either try to locate a position elsewhere in the university or community or create a new position within the department for your partner. This may involve using a position designed for some other purpose; at a minimum, it entails dedicating scarce resources to your partner. Some administrators have been known to offer a department extra funds or a future faculty position in exchange for hiring an applicant's partner. Although this may appear to be an ideal situation for you, you need to understand that, whether your partner is located in the same department as you or in a different department, he or she may likely become the "second fiddle," or an outsider who is perceived as being forced on the faculty. You can see why some administrators might want to avoid potential fallout from faculty or give up scarce resources, and might therefore be reluctant to pursue a position within the university for your partner aggressively. When your partner is not judged to be worth the effort required, when there is too much fallout from aggressively finding her or him a position in the university, or when the resources are not available, your entire deal may fall through. University administrators have walked away from very desirable faculty candidates at all ranks and levels because the human and economic costs became greater than the potential benefits.

POSSIBLE DUAL ACADEMIC
CAREER SOLUTIONS

It might appear at first glance that applying to a large university in a large urban area where there are other academic institutions might be the best route. This is not necessarily the case, though. Granted, the likelihood of finding two open positions in the appropriate academic areas may be greater than in less populated locations or smaller institutions. Some small liberal arts colleges and larger institutions in nonmetropolitan or rural areas may be more amenable to negotiating with dual career couples as a strategy to attract faculty and compete with their urban counterparts. If you prematurely rule out such areas or institutions, you might be closing the door to a host of opportunities.

If both you and your partner are academics, you will need to face the possibility of there not being two tenure-earning academic positions available. In this case, your partner (for whom there is no ideal position available) might agree to part-time employment, to a nonteaching position (e.g., clinical or research associate), or to pursue postdoctoral studies for a few years until a position becomes available. If you have the same specialization area, you might try to negotiate sharing the one available position.

PROBLEMS ARISING FOR
MIXED CAREER COUPLES

If your partner is a nonacademic and you are seeking the employing institution's help in securing employment for him or her, you should be aware that in almost all instances, the college or university has no control over hiring outside its purview. Realistically, you can expect that even the most sensitive, helpful institutions will be limited to passing along your partner's vita or resume, putting in a good word, or basically trying to grease the wheels for your partner. Even these efforts may be unproductive, depending on the area's job market and what is currently available. Of course, you have little to lose when asking for such assistance if you understand the university's limitations in these outside hirings, and do not make unrealistic demands or requests. To avoid problems and disappointment, you should be sure to make contingency plans in the event that job offers for your partner are not forthcoming. You would not want to be left in the unfortunate position of having to turn down an offer or have it fall through due solely to your partner's lack of employment.

POSSIBLE MIXED
CAREER SOLUTIONS

If your partner is in a highly specialized field, for instance, aeronautical design and engineering, you may find it impossible to find suitable employment in some areas. Therefore, you and your partner may have to consider the possibility of temporary or permanent career shifts, establishing a reserve savings for extended job searches, or agreeing to a time-limited commuter relationship. Some partners have used these employment challenges to begin a new graduate degree, move from government employment to private industry or vice versa, or establish their own businesses. Obviously, these decisions will require clear communication and critical negotiation between you and your partner as to what is mutually acceptable.

ESTABLISHING
YOUR BOTTOM LINE

In considering different available options, whether for dual academic or mixed career couples, you should think through these options and decide on your "bottom line," that is, your absolutely minimally acceptable positions, before you apply to any institution. Dual career employment issues often involve as much negotiation and compromise between the partners as they do between the job applicant and the university. For example, one couple may immediately accept the possibility that it may have commuter relationships, whereas you and your partner would immediately reject this option as unacceptable. Issues related to job salary and other job conditions, such as full time, part time, tenure earning, or not, need to be discussed by between you and your partner. You might decide to take a hard line initially, such as both of you requiring tenure earning positions in the same university or no deal, but be willing to accept a less desirable alternative if necessary. Consider your options very carefully, because you should not close off any options too prematurely because they might later become acceptable and eventually lead to satisfying positions.

APPROACHING THE INSTITUTION
WITH YOUR NEEDS

If you are being pursued by an institution, it is a good idea to be up front from the beginning about dual career issues and job preferences or needs for your partner. Administrators often require considerable time to work out different kinds of arrangements. Being up front does not mean that you should phrase your requirements or preferences in the form of a demand. Demanding or aggressive approaches, as opposed to direct, assertive approaches, tend to be interpreted as indicators of future faculty problematic behavior, whereas the latter usually come across as more reasonable requests or bits of information. Consider the following:

> I'm interested in your position but I won't come unless you can get my husband a job in the biology department.

versus

> I'm interested in your position and I want to tell you that my husband is seeking a faculty position in biology as well.

You might be surprised to learn how many job candidates seem to approach the dual career job hunt from the first fairly aggressive position. Although you might have decided not to go to a place where your partner does not get a job, you should still present yourself as interested in the position and willing to work out the problem. Administrators will be much more likely to go the extra mile for you and your partner if you do not enter the process with a demanding, hostile attitude. Even though you may not intend to communicate aggressiveness or hostility, the administrator or search committee member may get that message. This approach may serve as a red flag, and immediately reduce the likelihood of a successful outcome.

SAME SEX COUPLES

Our discussion so far has applied evenly to heterosexual and same sex couples in the job market. An important and unfortunate exception, however, relates to biases that continue to exist on some U.S. campuses and in some departments against homosexually oriented people. In the face of this type of bias, if you are a member of a same sex couple, you will need to decide just how open you will be about your partner and your partner's job requirements. Some individuals decide to be as open as possible with the notion that if biases exist, they would rather know about them up front, before deciding to take a job at a particular institution. If you choose this approach, you should recognize that this openness may eliminate you from some institutions' consideration; you must decide if the desire for openness is stronger than the desire for particular job possibilities.

Many same sex couples limit their job searches to larger metropolitan areas and to institutions where the likelihood of bias is known to be minimal or nonexistent. If you are a new job candidate and are unsure about the appropriate degree of openness for you and your partner, you might choose the "don't ask, don't tell" approach. Be aware, however, that there are two risks involved in this approach. First, depending on the institution and the individuals involved, you may be left to your own resourcefulness in securing a job for your partner without any assistance from the institution. Second, if the relationship eventually becomes known to others in the department or university, you may be subject to their biases. Weigh the pros and cons of each approach, recognizing that this is a very personal type of decision, and remembering never to underestimate the ignorance of the highly educated, especially when it comes to issues of sexual orientation.

Two Searches—Two Outcomes

Anna W. was nearing the end of her doctoral studies. Her husband, Bob, had graduated 2 years earlier with a law degree, and was currently employed at a large law firm. They had decided that, because neither of them had any particular connection to the community in which they were now living, they would consider moving to whatever location offered the best opportunity for both of them. Although they felt they did not require help from an institution in finding work for Bob, they decided to use the institution's willingness as an indication of how much it wanted Anna.

Anna looked through the *Chronicle of Higher Education* and spoke with the members of her dissertation committee to let them know that she was looking for work. Within a short time, she had uncovered 13 attractive possibilities, and had sent each copies of her curriculum vitae and cover letters indicating interest in interviewing at the coming national conference. She did not mention to any of them that she was married, or that she would need help in finding a position for her husband, preferring to talk about this in a face-to-face interview in which she would feel more comfortable selling her qualifications and her willingness to work cooperatively with the institution toward that end.

At each of the six brief face-to-face interviews at this conference, Anna answered all the questions put to her about her areas of interest and her experience, allowing the search committee to satisfy its curiosity about her qualifications and begin to make judgments about how she would fit. Then, in the last part of the interviews, when committee members asked her if she had questions, she brought up the fact that she was married, and asked the search committee what sort of job opportunities it felt might be in the community. She let it know that her husband was comfortable about the prospect of finding employment on his own, but that the more important matter was how well she and the institution fit together. Although this was not altogether true, she felt that it would be better at this time not to make demands.

Three weeks after her interviews at the conference, three of the six schools contacted her and asked her to come to on-campus interviews. Before going to the interviews, she carefully looked into the demographics of each area, and she and her husband discussed the pros and cons. When she went on the interviews, Anna carefully explored the attitudes of the faculty about their willingness to help find work for her husband. She asked faculty in her individual interviews if they had had the problem of finding employment for a spouse to ascertain how much energy the school might be willing to expend on this problem. She asked the secretary to copy the yellow pages to see how many law firms were located in the area. One of the institutions showed very little interest in helping her out. She found the faculty to be rather cool to her, and sensed a lack of genuine interest in her. Therefore, when she returned home, she discussed it with her husband, and they decided to let the university politely know that she was no longer interested in the position.

The second school was a small liberal arts college in a very small town located about 40 miles away from a major city. It was a beautiful area, full of history, and a wonderful place to raise children. Because there were only two law firms in the town, however, Bob would probably have a long daily commute if a position could be found somewhere in the city.

The third school was a large university where she could really do the research she had been dreaming of. Faculty clearly liked her, and she felt that she fit in well there. The city was large enough that there probably would be numerous job opportunities in the area for Bob.

To Anna's delight, both the small college and the large university called her with offers. In negotiating with them, Anna was very up front about her husband's needs. She asked how they would be able to help her, thinking that the small college would probably be able to do nothing toward helping Bob. She even apologized to the dean for asking for help because she knew how much trouble it would be, but explained that she really wanted to work there and would try to work with the school in some way. To her great surprise, the small college indicated that it would look aggressively into ways to find some sort of employment for her husband, whereas the large university felt that she and Bob should handle the problem on their own.

Several days later, the dean of the small college called and said that he thought he would be able to ensure Bob an interview for a management position in a local department store. It was not a law position, but it would bring in more money than Bob was making at his law firm, and would give them time to find something more to his liking if he found he wanted to look elsewhere. Anna accepted the position.

Compare the scenario shown above with the following story of Bert and Sarah R.

As a marine biologist, Bert knew that the number of schools available to him would be rather limited. Sarah, who was 6 months pregnant with their first child, had a PhD in psychology and was currently employed at the university at which Bert was getting his doctorate. Like Anna, Bert told his dissertation committee that he was looking for work, searched the professional newspapers and journals, and set up interviews with several schools at the national conference. Also like Anna, he did not tell anyone that he was married or that his wife would need employment after their baby was born. Unlike Anna, however, Bert did not mention his needs at the brief interviews at the conference, or even at the on-campus interviews he was able to get with three schools. Instead, he waited until he had job offers from two of the three, thinking that he would be able to play them off against each other.

When the schools called, Bert told each of them that he would be interested in working there, but only if they would find a place for his wife either in that university or in one within the same city. He also told each that the other was interested in him and working with him on this problem of employment for his wife. As it happened, one of the schools did have an opening in its psychology department for a junior faculty position. The other school had nothing, and immediately withdrew its offer. With the withdrawal of this offer, Bert was left with only one choice, and no way to play schools off against each other.

The search committee at the remaining university was angered that Bert had not mentioned his wife during their interviews. It had identified two other candidates who had been open and above-board with their needs and who were almost as well qualified as Bert. Because it did have a junior faculty position open in the university's psychology department, however, and it did like his credentials, it went on to negotiate with Bert. At that point, Bert had to mention that Sarah was 6 months pregnant and would need to take maternity leave shortly after their arrival. At this point, the director of the unit expressed regret that the school would be unable to accommodate Bert, and withdrew the job offer.

The two main differences between Bert and Anna were their flexibility and their openness. Anna and her husband were able and willing to move, and to accommodate the peculiarities and opportunities within their favorite institution's location. They were open and honest about their needs without being demanding. Bert was too cocky, too sure of himself, and left no room to maneuver. His lack of openness and his demanding attitude alienated the institutions, lost him a job, and earned him a reputation that will follow him.

SUMMARY

This chapter has taken a realistic look at the kinds of issues that dual career couples face in the academic job market. Many couples have been successful, and more couples will continue to be successful, in their search for the ideal faculty positions. You should have several contingency plans when you enter the job market, however, and a mind set of not closing any doors on employment possibilities (or location or size of institution) before you have fully explored their possibilities. The more flexible you can be, the better the possibilities. You and your partner need to negotiate your needs before applying anywhere. Realistically assess how your needs fit in with the needs of institutions you are interested in and the demographics of the areas in which the institutions are found.

Keep in mind, too, not to look or act desperate, even though you both may be feeling that way, and be careful that you are not perceived as being arrogant or demanding in your request for assistance in finding placement for your partner. Finally, remember that the academic job market is largely still a sellers' market, and therefore many institutions are willing to work with you and your partner in solving your problem.

CONCLUDING REMARKS

We may be biased, but we feel that an academic position is one of the best jobs in the world. Most campuses are physically attractive environments; the landscaping and architecture are often unique and interesting, and may be full of history and meaning. For the most part, academic life allows you the job freedom to think, say, and research whatever you choose. Not only do you enjoy relative freedom, but you are also immersed in an environment rich with the spirit of inquiry. Perhaps it is best said by a long-term academic and university president: "The essence of academic life is the opportunity—indeed, the demand—for continual investment in oneself. It is a unique chance for a lifetime of building and renewing intellectual capital" (Rosovsky, 1990). We experience this through research and knowledge building, satisfying intellectual curiosity, and teaching and mentoring students, forever reaping the satisfactions of their accomplishments. Only a handful of jobs provide the opportunity to influence so many, whether it be through research, teaching, or service.

The academic life is certainly not for everyone. But for those who aspire to be academics, we encourage you to follow your dream! Our hope is that by reading this book, you will find some useful information that will help you locate the academic position that will allow you to fulfill that dream.

EPILOGUE

What If You Can't Find an Academic Position?

BRUCE A. THYER

A happy note for displaced academics is that studies show that PhDs who have gone into administration, government, or business actually have greater job satisfaction than those who are college teachers.

—Wyman & Risser, 1983

OK. You read this book months ago and followed all its sage advice. You sought counsel and assistance from your major professor, committee members, departmental chair, faculty, and others equally uninterested in your career aspirations, all to no avail! Try as you might, you have not been offered an acceptable tenure-track position in the type of academic institution you wish to spend your career in. After all your hard work and obvious talent, how could this have happened?

There are a number of considerations. Dispassionately examine the brutal possibility that you are simply not a competitive candidate. Maybe your graduate student teaching evaluations were poor, or your areas of scholarship are too circumscribed. Perhaps the job market is glutted with eager new PhDs in your field. Perhaps your academic institution is not a very highly rated one in your field. Has word gotten out (from departmental faculty, fellow graduates) that you are difficult to work with, a bigot, a sexist? In some fields, white males are actively discriminated against in terms of hiring decisions. The role of simple chance, of not being in the right place at the right time for the right job, cannot be excluded.

None of the above factors need permanently preclude your entry into academia. Witness the numbers of current faculty who are poor teachers, are from mediocre institutions, have narrow interests, are sexist, and so on! What are your options? Here are a few.

DELAY FORMAL GRADUATION

For most graduate students, there is a significant time delay between when they defend their dissertation and when they walk through the formal graduation ceremony arranged by the university and receive the diploma. As a practical matter, you are a "doctor" once you have defended. Sometimes your department can provide a letter to your prospective employers stating that you have passed your doctoral defense. It may be possible for you to delay formally applying for graduation after defending your dissertation, and to remain a "student" for another term or two, perhaps as a graduate assistant of some sort. This time could be used to enhance your instructional credentials and to polish up your dissertation research for publication (something you will find little opportunity to do as a full-time assistant professor). Wrap up some other scholarly projects or undertake new, short-term ones with faculty. If being a graduate or teaching assistant entitles you to a tuition waiver, consider taking another course or two to gain further knowledge in your field.

Retaining the role of graduate student for a while provides you with a continuing niche in society. You maintain the link with the university culture and resources (e.g., student discounts, library, gym facilities) that may be closed to you once you officially graduate. And you avoid the stigma of being unemployed and of having to explain to your parents why you do not have a job after all this time.

HONESTLY ASSESS YOUR PERSONAL CHARACTERISTICS

Watch some videos of yourself teaching a class or interacting with others. What do you look like? If you have some distinctive mannerism, affectation, dress, or other characteristic that is perceived by others as unattractive or bizarre and is correctable, consider doing what you can to amend it. Even if you are very proud of your tattoos or pierced body parts, consider covering them up or removing the rings and chains when interviewing for a position. If you are a male, a very bushy beard, nasal stud, or dual pigtails a la Willie Nelson may have no objective bearing on your ability to teach accounting, but these features may (unfair though it may be) turn off search committees. Now may be the time to spend a couple of hundred dollars to remove that conspicuous facial mole, or to replace your gold incisor with a conventional cap. One doctoral student I know deliberately keeps his hair at one eighth of an inch long all over his head. This is a great guy and a talented professional, but I suspect that come job interview time, his resemblance to a member of the Aryan Brotherhood may work against him. I hope that he acquires a more conventional hairstyle when he nears graduation.

Some things you cannot change, so don't fret about them. Those that can be altered should be, at least until you receive an acceptable job offer. Drop a few pounds if you are overweight, or add a few if you are too thin. If your hours in the library have left you as pale as an extra from *Night of the Living Dead,* get a little sun. Drop the grunge look in favor of a Harris Tweed jacket or the ubiquitous navy blue suit. Shed the Doc Martens for dress shoes, or at least highly polished slip-ons. Pretend to conform.

THE ADJUNCT PART-TIME
FACULTY ROUTE

In 1970, about 22% of postsecondary education faculty were in nontenure-track positions. This increased to about 50% of all college and university faculty in 1992 (Pratt, Courteau, Gluck, Kasper, Swonger, Thompson, & Benjamin, 1992). The use of part-time and adjunct faculty is rapidly growing in higher education. This means that you may be more successful seeking adjunct, part-time, or temporary positions than a more competitive full-time tenure track appointment. There is actually a minor industry of doctorates who float from position to position, teaching one course at University X and another at College Y, or take a half-time 1-year position someplace else, all the while continuing to apply for a full-time, tenure-track position (FTTTP).

This is not a desirable state of affairs, but it should seriously be considered as an option to unemployment or to working outside your field once you have graduated. The application process is similar. Seek out such openings, and submit your cover letter and CV. If you are interviewed, put your best foot forward, be enthusiastic, and in general apply all the recruitment tools described throughout this book. Whether the job involves teaching a single undergrad class in your field or more intensive responsibilities, do the very best you can to build on the experience, and add it to your CV. Perhaps get the departmental chair to provide you with a glowing letter of recommendation or network with the full-timers in seeking assistance with your job search.

THE POSTDOCTORAL
FELLOWSHIP ROUTE

In many disciplines, particularly in the hard sciences, students commonly complete one or more years of a postdoctoral fellowship. Here you are neither fish nor fowl, not a graduate student any longer but not a full-fledged faculty member either. Postdoc positions typically pay a good deal less than a FTTTP, and the fringe benefits may be more limited. On the plus side, they provide (at least the good ones do) the opportunity to gain additional research or practice experience, add to your publications, expand your professional network of friends and associates, perhaps gain some teaching experience, and remain active in your field.

In some disciplines, postdocs are extremely competitive, whereas in others, such appointments go begging for applicants. They are usually time limited, 1 to 2 years being the most common, at which point the FTTTP search begins anew, leaving you to face the problems of relocating and the like once again. Your postdoc may have made you a more competitive applicant.

THE SOFT-MONEY ROUTE

University budgets are composed of hard funds (e.g., state appropriated) and soft funds (e.g., external grants). Soft money is typically awarded to university departments after one or more faculty write a grant, applying for funding to support projects in research, training, or service. Such grant-based projects often contain money to pay for one or more so-called soft-money positions. Sometimes these have titles such as "project director" and "director of training," and sometimes they are more generic, such as "statistical consultant" and "computer analyst." These jobs can be half or full time, in most cases. While you are completing your graduate degree, if the academic job prospects look grim, consider working with one or more faculty in the preparation of an externally funded grant, which, if funded, would provide you with a job for the duration of the grant, usually 1 or more years. The pluses are obvious—possibly a position, and definitely some valuable experience in preparing and submitting a grant (an esoteric art in itself).

While employed in a soft-money position such as this, you can garner valuable work experience, and perhaps accrue some publications, while you gear up for another year of applications and recruitment efforts, still attempting to land that FTTTP. Usually the pay and benefits (health insurance, retirement, and the like) associated with a soft-money position are comparable to those obtained by personnel funded with hard money.

The downside is that grant work can be fairly high-pressure stuff, conducted under great time constraints, and in many fields the prospects of funding are low due to intense competition. You could spend much time on Professor Grimshaw's grant application, hoping that if Grimshaw is funded she will keep her word and hire you as the project director. If the project is funded, Grimshaw may hire someone else (it has been known to happen!). If it is not funded, all your time and effort have gone for naught. Also, such soft-money positions may not involve teaching in your field. If you are looking for a FTTTP teaching at the college or university level, this can be a negative factor to consider.

TEACH ABROAD

Another common route for unemployed academics is to teach abroad, either in your field or in a related one, or something generic such as English as a Second Language or American Studies. Many foreign institutions welcome short-term stays from recent PhDs. One chap I know left an assistant professor position in the South and immediately became a full professor and dean of graduate studies at a private college in the Far East, with a 3-year contract. In Hong Kong, for example, new assistant professors in my field, social work, start at about $70,000 a year, plus generous benefits, including a housing allowance. The *Chronicle of Higher Education, Science,* and other periodicals contain advertisements for foreign academic appointments. The Fulbright Scholarship program and similar programs sponsored by governmental or nongovernmental organizations (e.g., the Japan Society, Alliance Francaise, the Goethe Society) are other routes to a temporary position teaching abroad.

WORK IN THE BUSINESS SECTOR

Here I am talking about working in your field, perhaps a bit tangentially, within the private sector. There need not be any stigma attached to this. Indeed, many of the most talented products of graduate or professional schooling actively seek this option (e.g., see Arron, 1991; Bestor, 1982; Wyman & Risser, 1983). Peterson's (1996) ubiquitous guide to obtaining work in the business sector is a good resource to explore this option. The MA or PhD in English may find a good position in the publishing industry. My cousin has a law degree, and his expertise in both Japanese and Arabic make him a valued counsel for foreign businesses. Those with graduate degrees in the computer sciences and a few other selected fields will find that an academic position will likely pay considerably less than positions in the private sector. My own university finds it difficult to recruit and retain academics in computer sciences because these folks are constantly being lured away to the private sector. The private sector affords less scope for those trained in some academic disciplines than others, although the scene is constantly changing. An emerging field called "applied sociology" is dedicated to activist-type intervention in social problems, as opposed to merely academically studying them. Similarly, there is a new area called "philosophical counseling," in which individuals academically trained in the discipline of philosophy open up private practices providing counseling services for those wrestling with existential and other philosophical matters (as opposed to mental health concerns).

Individuals with advanced degrees in a foreign language can often find lucrative opportunities in translation services, those skilled in two or more foreign languages even more (see DeGalan & Lambert, 1994).

Many graduate programs sponsor one or more job fairs each year. During these events, prospective employers set up booths and display brochures extolling the virtues of working for the Veeblefitzer Corporation, and personnel officers are there to meet with applicants and to conduct preliminary interviews. In some fields (e.g., business, law), these are very big, formal events, and in others, they are more generic, less-structured affairs, not discipline specific. Find out if and when your graduate or professional school sponsors such a job fair, put on your suit and a smile, and attend. If there are other schools nearby, consider attending their job fairs as well.

WORK FOR THE
FEDERAL GOVERNMENT

Words cannot do justice to the employment possibilities available with the U.S. federal government! For example, take the field of law enforcement (see Warner, 1992). There is the Federal Bureau of Investigation; the Central Intelligence Agency; the Bureau of Alcohol, Tobacco, and Drugs; the Secret Service; the National Security Agency; the Internal Revenue Service; the Fish and Wildlife Service; the Department of Justice; the Environmental Protection Agency; the Occupational Safety and Health Administration; and the Bureau of Engraving and Printing, to name a few. Many of these agencies have positions for professional lawyers, chemists, statisticians, managers, physicians, diversity consultants, engineers, biologists, economists, accountants, and so forth. The same could be said for the various cabinet-level organizations, the departments of Commerce, Labor, Education, Health and Human Resources (the National Institute of Health alone employs an army of graduate professionals in dozens of fields).

Federal positions typically offer very good job security, good initial starting salaries for graduate-level professionals, terrific benefits, and a structured career ladder permitting one to rise to his or her level of competence. On the downside, annual promotions are often low, sometimes limited to cost of living. But this is not uncommon in academia too, so perhaps it is not a salient factor.

WORK FOR A STATE GOVERNMENT

What I said above regarding the federal government is replicated at the state level, which offers a wide variety of positions, competitive

pay and benefits, secure retirement programs, and the like. Most
federal departments have state counterparts and a civil service or merit
system for recruiting that you will need to link up with. Fill out the
forms accurately and submit them. In most places, you will be auto-
matically notified of openings for which you may be qualified, while
at the same time prospective employers will be sent your application
materials. To some extent, many state roles are being privatized to
entrepreneurial companies. Texas, for example, is assigning almost all
public welfare services (eligibility determinations, work-training, and
the like) to private corporations; Georgia, in common with many
states, is contracting out some of its prisons. These job losses in
services traditionally provided by the state are offset to some extent
by corresponding growth in the private sector, but often salaries are
lower, less skilled individuals are hired, and the number of positions
is smaller.

JOIN THE MILITARY

The U.S. armed forces provide an amazing array of vocational positions, some field related and some unrelated. I know of one accounting
major who became an officer in the Army's tank corps. Just about
every conceivable professional or graduate school major has a coun-
terpart in the military. The U.S. Army employs veterinarians and
musicians, mathematicians and statisticians, chaplains and chemists.
No matter what field your degree is in, it is worth talking to a recruiter
from one or more of the armed forces about becoming a commissioned
officer. A phone call will elicit voluminous information in the mail,
and you will likely be surprised at the choices available. Consider both
the major uniformed forces (Army, Navy, Air Force, Marine Corps)
and the less-known branches (Coast Guard, U.S. Public Health Service). With a graduate degree, you will likely go in as a first lieutenant
or captain in the Army, Air Force, or Marines or an ensign in the Navy.
Officer training will not be particularly physically onerous (except for
the Marines), and it may be intellectually interesting. Pay and benefits

are competitive in many fields, and the opportunities for travel and additional training are generous.

WORK IN A FIELD UNRELATED
TO YOUR DEGREE

I will not devote much time to the tactics of finding a regular, nonacademic job in the private sector. The folklore about PhD taxi drivers and waitresses in New York City is demoralizing enough. A particularly flexible arrangement worth considering is working for a temporary employment agency. You get listed on its roster, enumerating what you can do (e.g., word processing, computer spreadsheets), and when you can do it (e.g., weekdays 8 to 6, evenings only, weekends). As the temp agency is contacted by prospective employers, if there is a match between your abilities and availability and the posted job, it will call, offering the position. Sometimes such jobs can last for months, and some agencies even offer benefits. If a temp job turns out to be dreadful, you can walk away. Justice (1994) and Baratz (1995) provide good guides to obtaining temporary employment along these lines.

CONSIDER VOLUNTEER WORK

The United States has a long tradition of volunteerism, and the president recently made an impassioned plea for citizens to become more involved in charitable work. Unable to find a suitable academic appointment, you could make a virtue out of a vice by affiliating with some form of structured voluntary service program, in which your graduate skills could be put to good use in a charitable or philanthropic endeavor, either in the United States or abroad. The Peace Corps is still recruiting folks, and it provides language and cultural training before sending you off to a developing country to instruct indigenous people on how to improve their lives. There is a pervasive need for teachers at all levels, and plenty of room for people with differing academic backgrounds to contribute something related to one's field. You get some say-so in determining where you will go and what you will do. Housing and food are provided, and a monthly stipend is paid, much of it when you leave the Peace Corps. Such experience can be seen by future academic employers as both excellent professional preparation (depending on what you actually did) and reflective of a noble character. Closer to home, the Volunteers in Service to America (VISTA) and AmeriCorps programs still exist, with thousands of volunteers spread across the country.

Considerable opportunity also exists for full-time volunteer work with various secular and religious organizations. Woodworth (1993) is an excellent resource to become informed about the prospects of this form of service. You may end up doing some good, perhaps enhance your professional skills, and be prepared after a year or so to launch out once more on the job-search enterprise. The Maryknoll nuns, Israeli kibbutzim, United Nations, Doctors Without Borders, Greenpeace, Habitat for Humanity, and International Red Cross are all examples of organizations that rely on the work of volunteers and, depending on your potential contributions, may welcome you with open arms.

A less altruistic option would be to undertake a religious retreat. Without joining holy orders yourself, a number of monasteries and similar organizations allow you to be secluded for varying periods of time. You provide some labor on behalf of the monastery, attend frequent religious services, and enjoy a quiet, low-stress life, the consolations of prayer and meditation, and the opportunity to spend your leisure moments in the library. Attending required matins before the sun is up may not be to everyone's taste, but if you are genuinely inclined in that direction, labeling this period of your life a "retreat" or "religious sabbatical" provides a face-saving justification for not being employed in a FTTTP (although such an experience may be excellent preparation for the academic life!).

GET ANOTHER DEGREE

It may sound strange, but another degree can be a very useful way to enhance one's marketability. Face it, some fields are swamped with

PhDs (e.g., the humanities), and in others, PhDs are in short supply. The laws of the marketplace are not suspended in the halls of academia. One fellow I know earned a PhD in philosophy from a prestigious private university in the Southeast. In vain he sought an FTTTP, taking a series of part-time and adjunct appointments, teaching a class here and one there, but never finding a settled home in an academic department of philosophy. After a few years, he decided to return to graduate school, and spent 18 months earning a master's of social work. With this in hand, he worked awhile at a state mental hospital, and with this experience, the MSW, and his PhD, he obtained a full-time teaching position in a 4-year college teaching human services.

In academic social work, for example, tenure-track assistant professors are typically required to have the MSW (a practice degree) and a doctorate in social work or a closely related field. This opens the door for individuals with a doctorate that proves to be unmarketable to spend a little more time in school, get the additional master's, and then be better leveraged to teach as a full-time faculty member. I have recommended this option for PhDs in psychology (see Thyer, 1989), and I know of lawyers and persons with doctorates in other fields doing the same thing. My own department is typical: Of 19 faculty in FTTTPs and with doctorates, only 9 have doctorates in social work. The balance have degrees in education, public administration, and other fields. Analogous situations exist in other fields.

Apart from earning another full-fledged graduate degree, consider obtaining additional training that falls short of this. For example, in academic psychology, the PhD trained in a nonpractice area (social psychology, experimental, developmental) can complete a so-called retread program in clinical psychology, involving additional course work and internship experiences. Once completed, licensure as a much more marketable clinical psychologist is possible, as is access to the more common academic FTTTPs available in clinical and counseling psychology. Some universities offer certificate programs in various fields or at summer research institutes to enable you to acquire advanced skills in statistics or other research methods. Completion of such programs may be the necessary additional step to land you the slot you want.

CHECK OUT THE CAREER PLANNING
AND PLACEMENT OFFICE ON CAMPUS

Just about all universities have a service called the Career Planning and Placement Office (CPPO). These are staffed with talented individuals whose purpose is to help the university's graduates find fulfilling professional employment. They offer free assistance in resume writing, enhancing one's interviewing skills, networking, and linking students with prospective employers, as well as a library on job-finding resources in various fields. Their success is measured by finding you a job.

Be aware that most CPPOs are oriented toward helping the swarms of undergraduates find positions, but they are more than ready to lend assistance to graduate and professional students as well. One common service they provide is to maintain a large library of three-ring binders, each prominently labeled with the name of a business firm or corporation, local, national, or international, containing current listing of job openings, contact persons, and the like. The CPPO at my university has a room lined with bookshelves containing hundreds of these binders. These are for you to use in developing job leads. They can also help you find Web sites on the Internet related to employment. For example, the classified employment ads of most major newspapers are now available on the Net.

If you, like me, have your heart set on a career as a university-based academic, I wish you well. If it does not immediately work out for you, you can quote Oscar Wilde's wry observation that "Everyone who is incapable of learning has taken to teaching." The recruiting of faculty has its seasons, and its highs and lows, all of which vary somewhat among the disciplines. By all means try again in another year, in another country, or in another field. Persistence will pay off. Good luck.

REFERENCES

Arron, D. L. (1991). *Running from the law: Why good lawyers are getting out of the legal profession.* Berkeley, CA: Ten Speed.

Baratz, L. R. (1995). *VGM's guide to temporary employment.* Chicago, IL: NTC.

Barbezat, D. A. (1992). The market for new PhD economists. *Journal of Economic Education, 23,* 262-276.

Bestor, D. K. (1982). *Aside from teaching, what in the world can you do?* Seattle: University of Washington Press.

Bowen, W. G., & Sosa, J. A. (1989). *Prospects for faculty in the arts and sciences: A study of factors affecting demand and supply, 1987-2012.* Princeton, NJ: Princeton University Press.

Burke, K. L. (1988). *A new academic market place.* New York: Greenwood.

Chesebro, J. W. (1991). Preparing for the future: Faculty development issues in the year 2000. *ACA Bulletin, 7,* 11-24.

Chronister, J. L., & Truesdell, T. C. (1991). Exploring faculty issues and institutional planning for the twenty-first century. *Review of Higher Education, 14,* 467-484.

Dalbey, M. A. (1995). What is a comprehensive university, and do I want to work there? *Association of Departments of English Bulletin, 111,* 14-16.

DeGalan, J., & Lambert, S. (1994). *Great jobs for foreign language majors.* Lincolnwood, IL: VGM Career Group.

Dewey, B. E., & Gardner, D. C. (1983). Do you really want to teach? Fifteen job search rules. *College Student Journal, 17,* 80-82.

Duell, O. K. (1994). Tenure and promotion: Questions to ask and strategies for success. *Mid-Western Educational Researcher, 7,* 15-19.

Feld, S. (1988). The academic market place in social work. *Journal of Social Work Education, 24,* 201-211.

Formo, D. M. (1995, March). *Becoming literate in the employment line: Graduate students' strategies for job placement.* Paper presented at the annual meeting of the Conference on College Composition and Communication, Washington, DC.

Gaus, P. J., Sledge, A. C., & Joels, A. R. (1983). The academic interview. *Journal of College Placement, 43,* 61-62.

Gibbs, P., & Locke, B. (1989). Tenure and promotion in accredited graduate social work programs. *Journal of Social Work Education, 25,* 126-130.

Gill, J. I., (1992). *Bringing into focus the factors affecting faculty supply and demand.* Boulder, CO: Western Commission for Higher Education. (ERIC Document Reproduction Service No. ED370471)

Harrison, D., & Sowers-Hoag, K. M. (1992, October). *Faculty recruitment and retention in schools of social work.* Paper presented at the annual conference of the Group for the Advancement of Doctoral Education, Pittsburgh, PA.

Harrison, D., Sowers-Hoag, K. M., & Gerdes, K. (1991). *Recent faculty hires in social work: Trends and implications for academia.* Paper presented at the Council on Social Work Education annual program meeting, New Orleans.

Harrison, D., Sowers-Hoag, K. M., & Postley, B. J. (1989). Faculty hiring in social work: Dilemmas for educators or job candidates? *Journal of Social Work Education, 25,* 117-125.

Harrison, D., Sowers-Hoag, K. M., & Postley, B. J. (1989, March). *Recent faculty hires in social work: Trends and implications for academia.* Paper presented at the annual program meeting of the Council on Social Work Education, New Orleans.

Iacono, W. G. (1981). The academic job search: The experiences of a new PhD in the job market. *Canadian Psychology, 22,* 217-227.

Justice, P. O. (1994). *The temp track.* Princeton, NJ: Peterson's.

Kennedy, J. L., & Morrow, T. J. (1995). *Electronic job search revolution: How to win the new technology that's reshaping today's market.* New York: John Wiley.

Klesges, R. C., Sanchez, V. C., & Stanton, A. L. (1982). Obtaining employment in academia: The hiring process and characteristics of successful applicants. *Professional Psychology, 13,* 577-587.

Klingner, D. E., & Nalbandian, J. (1985). *Public personnel management: Contexts and strategies.* Englewood Cliffs, NJ: Prentice Hall.

Kogan, M., Moses, I., & El-Khawas, E. (1994). *Staffing higher education: Meeting new challenges.* Bristol, PA: Jessica Kingsley.

Lawhon, T., & Ennis, D. L. (1995). Recruiting and selecting community college faculty. *Community College Journal of Research and Practice, 19,* 349-359.

McDowell, E. E. (1987). Perceptions of the ideal cover letter and ideal resume. *Journal of Technical Writing and Communication, 17,* 179-191.

Minner, S., Ellsworth, J., & Prater, G. (1994). Experiences of applicants for college and university positions in special education. *Teacher Education and Special Education, 17,* 200-210.

Mooney, C. (1990, Feb. 7). New U.S. survey assembles a statistical portrait of the American professorate. *Chronicle of Higher Education,* p. A15.

Morgan, J. (1993). New study portends bad news for minority students and faculty. *Black Issues in Higher Education, 12,* 16-17.

Perlman, B. (1976). The hunt: Job hunting for the new PhD psychologist. *American Psychologist, 31,* 298-302.

116   FINDING AN ACADEMIC JOB

Peterson, M. W., & White, T. H. (1992). Faculty and administrator perceptions of their environments: Different views or different models of organization. *Research in Higher Education, 33,* 177-204.

Peterson's. (1996). *Job opportunities in business.* Princeton, NJ: Author.

Pratt, L. R., Courteau, J., Gluck, S., Kasper, H., Swonger, A. K., Thompson, K., & Benjamin, E. (1992). Report on the status of non-tenure-track faculty. *Academe, 78*(6), 39-48.

Reed, C. (1995, March). *So you want to teach at the two-year college: The application process.* Paper presented at the annual meeting of the Conference on College Composition and Communication, Washington, DC.

Rosovsky, H. (1990). *The university: An owner's manual.* New York: Norton.

Schuman, S. (1995). Small is . . . different. In A. L. Deneff & C. D. Goodwin (Eds.), *The academic handbook* (pp. 17-28). Durham, NC: Duke University Press.

Sheldon, P. J., & Collison, F. M. (1990). Faculty review criteria in tourism and hospitality. *Annals of Tourism Research, 17,* 556-567.

Shetty, S. (1995). The job market: An overview. In A. L. Deneff & C. D. Goodwin (Eds.), *The academic handbook* (pp. 128-135). Durham, NC: Duke University Press.

Showalter, E. (1985). *A career guide for PhDs and PhD candidates in English and foreign languages.* New York: Modern Language Association of America.

Sowers-Hoag, K. M., Harrison, D. F., & Dziegielewski, S. (1989, March). *Securing employment in social work education: Recent experiences of job candidates.* Paper presented at the annual program meeting of the Council on Social Work Education, Chicago.

Sudzina, M. R. (1991, February). *Evaluation of applicants for employment in higher education: A search committee's screening and selection criteria.* Paper presented at the annual meeting of the Mid-Western Educational Research Association, Chicago.

Teevan, J., Pepper, S., & Pellizzarti, J. (1992). Academic employment decisions and gender. *Research in Higher Education, 33,* 141-160.

Thyer, B. A. (1989). Social work: Professional opportunities for behavior analysts. *The Behavior Analyst, 12,* 89-91.

Thyer, B. A. (1994). *Successful publishing in scholarly journals.* Newbury Park, CA: Sage.

Tolbert, P. S., & Oberfield, A. A. (1991). Sources of organizational demography: Faculty sex ratios in colleges and universities. *Sociology of Education, 64,* 305-315.

Warner, J. W. (1992). *Federal jobs in law enforcement.* New York: Macmillan.

Wilbur, H. M. (1993). On getting a job. In A. L. Deneff & C. D. Goodwin (Eds.), *The academic handbook* (pp. 115-127). Durham, NC: Duke University Press.

Whitfield, T., & Weaver, J. (1991). *The demand of teacher education faculty: Some factors influencing employment.* (ERIC Document Reproduction Service No. ED336339)

Woodworth, D. (1993). *International directory of voluntary work.* Princeton, NJ: Peterson's.

Wyman, R. E., & Risser, N. A. (1983). *Humanities PhDs and non-academic careers.* Evanston, IL: Committee on Institutional Cooperation.

INDEX

ABOUT THE AUTHORS

Dianne F. Harrison is Dean of and Professor in the Florida State University School of Social Work. She received her PhD from the George Warren Brown School of Social Work, Washington University. She was the 1996 recipient of the George Warren Brown School of Social Work Distinguished Alumni Award. She has recently coauthored articles in *Family Planning Perspectives* and *Research on Social Work Practice* and is the coauthor of *Cultural Diversity and Social Work Practice* (2nd ed.). Her areas of expertise include behavior therapy, prevention research, marriage and family counseling, clinical research, and human sexuality. She is a member of the Board of Directors of the National Association of Deans and Directors in Social Work and is Chair of the Florida Association of Social Work Deans and Directors.

Karen Sowers-Hoag received her PhD in social work from Florida State University in 1986. She holds the appointments of Professor of Social Work and Dean of the College of Social Work at the University of Tennessee, Knoxville. Over the past decade, she and Dianne Harrison have conducted extensive research about the academic job market and have presented and published numerous manuscripts from their research. Sower-Hoag's other academic interests focus on children and families at risk, social work education, cultural diversity, and women's issues. She has served on the editorial boards of *Research on Social Work Practice* and *Journal of Applied Social Sciences.*